AQA A2
RELIGIOUS STUDIES
RELIGION AND ETHICS AND PHILOSOPHY OF RELIGION

my revision notes

AQA A2 RELIGIOUS STUDIES
RELIGION AND ETHICS AND PHILOSOPHY OF RELIGION

Peter Cole
Richard Gray

HODDER
EDUCATION

Richard Gray wishes to thank Nicola, Jack, Ethan, Elizabeth and Anna for their love and support.
Both authors also wish to thank the Hodder editing team for all their help, in particular Jane, Ruth, Caitlin and Vicky.

The publishers would like to thank the following for permission to reproduce copyright material:

Acknowledgements

Scripture quotations taken from The Holy Bible, New International Version Anglicised. Copyright © 1979, 1984 by Biblica, Inc. Used by permission of Hodder & Stoughton Publishers, a division of Hachette UK Ltd. All rights reserved. 'NIV' is a registered trademark of Biblica, Inc. UK trademark number 1448790; and Zondervan Publishing House, www.zondervan.com

Every effort has been made to trace all copyright holders, but if any have been inadvertently overlooked the Publishers will be pleased to make the necessary arrangements at the first opportunity.

Although every effort has been made to ensure that website addresses are correct at time of going to press, Hodder Education cannot be held responsible for the content of any website mentioned in this book. It is sometimes possible to find a relocated web page by typing in the address of the home page for a website in the URL window of your browser.

Hachette UK's policy is to use papers that are natural, renewable and recyclable products and made from wood grown in sustainable forests. The logging and manufacturing processes are expected to conform to the environmental regulations of the country of origin.

Orders:

Please contact Bookpoint Ltd, 130 Milton Park, Abingdon, Oxon OX14 4SB.
Telephone: +44 (0)1235 827720.
Fax: +44 (0)1235 400454.
Lines are open 9.00a.m.–5.00p.m., Monday to Saturday, with a 24-hour message answering service. Visit our website at www.hoddereducation.co.uk.

First published in 2013 by
Hodder Education,
an Hachette UK company
338 Euston Road
London NW1 3BH

Impression number 10 9 8 7 6 5 4 3 2
Year   2017 2016 2015 2014

Typeset in CronosPro-Lt 12/14 points by Datapage (India) Pvt. Ltd.
Printed and bound in Spain

A catalogue record for this title is available from the British Library
ISBN 978 1 444 182408

Get the most from this book

Everyone has to decide his or her own revision strategy, but it is essential to review your work, learn it and test your understanding. These Revision Notes will help you do that in a planned way, topic by topic. They cover the Ethics module (Unit 3A), the Philosophy of Religion module (Unit 3B), and two topics from the Religion and Human Experience module (Unit 4A – 'Life, death and beyond' and 'Religious experience'). Use this book as the cornerstone of your revision and don't hesitate to write in it – personalise your notes and check your progress by ticking off each section as you revise.

You can also keep track of your revision by ticking off each topic heading in the book. You may find it helpful to add your own notes as you work through each topic.

☑ Tick to track your progress

Use the revision planner on pages 4 and 5 to plan your revision, topic by topic. Tick each box when you have:

- revised and understood a topic
- tested yourself
- practised the exam questions and gone online to check your answers.

Features to help you succeed

Exam tips

Throughout the book there are tips to help you boost your final grade.

Typical mistakes

Identifies the typical mistakes candidates make.

Now test yourself

These short, knowledge-based questions provide the first step in testing your learning. Look up the answers at the back of this book.

Key words

Clear, concise definitions of essential key terms are provided on the page where they appear.

Key quotes

Quotations from key scholars concisely express key ideas or views relevant to each topic.

Exam practice

Practice exam questions are provided for each topic. Use them to consolidate your revision and practise your exam skills.

Online

Go online to check your answers to the exam questions at www.therevisionbutton.co.uk/myrevisionnotes

My revision planner

Unit 3B Philosophy of Religion

Unit 4A Religion and Human Experience

Assessment Objectives (AO)

For A2 Religious Studies you must sit **two** modules: one module must be from Unit 3 and one topic from Unit 4. The Unit 3 module has four questions of which you must answer any **two**. The Unit 4 topic has two questions of which you must answer **one**. Each question is divided into two parts. In both units the first part of the question assesses the Assessment Objective Knowledge and Understanding. The second part of the question assesses the Assessment Objective Evaluation. It is therefore important to be aware of the weighting for each Assessment Objective in each module.

In Unit 4, candidates are expected to demonstrate knowledge and understanding of the connections between different elements of their course of study.

Assessment Objectives		Unit	Marks	Module weighting (%)
AO1	Knowledge and Understanding	3	30 marks	60%
AO2	Evaluation	3	20 marks	40%
AO1	Knowledge and Understanding	4	45 marks	60%
AO2	Evaluation	4	30 marks	40%

Exam practice answers at **www.therevisionbutton.co.uk/myrevisionnotes**

Countdown to my exams

6–8 weeks to go

- Start by looking at the specification available from **www.aqa.org.uk**. Make sure you know exactly what material you need to revise and the style of the examination. Use the revision planner on pages 4 and 5 to familiarise yourself with the topics.
- Organise your notes, making sure you have covered everything on the specification. The revision planner will help you group your notes into topics.
- Work out a realistic revision plan that will allow you time for relaxation. Set aside days and times for all the subjects that you need to study, and stick to your timetable.
- Set yourself sensible targets. Break your revision down into focused sessions of around 40 minutes, divided by breaks. These Revision Notes organise the basic facts into short, memorable sections to make revising easier.

Revised ☐

4–6 weeks to go

- Read through the relevant sections of this book and refer to the exam tips, typical mistakes and key terms. Tick off the topics as you feel confident about them. Highlight those topics you find difficult and look at them again in detail.
- Test your understanding of each topic by working through the 'Now test yourself' questions in the book. Look up the answers in the Answers section on pages 106–109.
- Make a note of any problem areas as you revise, and ask your teacher to go over these in class.
- Look at past papers. They are one of the best ways to revise and practise your exam skills. Write or prepare planned answers to the exam practice questions provided in this book. Check your answers online at **www.therevisionbutton.co.uk/myrevisionnotes**
- Try different revision methods. For example, you can make notes using mind maps, spider diagrams or flashcards.
- Track your progress using the revision planner and give yourself a reward when you have achieved your target.

Revised ☐

One week to go

- Try to fit in at least one more timed practice of an entire past paper and seek feedback from your teacher, comparing your work closely with the mark scheme.
- Check the revision planner to make sure you haven't missed out any topics. Brush up on any areas of difficulty by talking them over with a friend or getting help from your teacher.
- Attend any revision classes put on by your teacher. Remember, he or she is an expert at preparing people for examinations.

Revised ☐

The day before the examination

- Flick through these Revision Notes for useful reminders, for example the exam tips, typical mistakes and key terms.
- Check the time and place of your examination.
- Make sure you have everything you need – extra pens and pencils, tissues, a watch, bottled water, sweets.
- Allow some time to relax and have an early night to ensure you are fresh and alert for the examinations.

Revised ☐

My exams

A2 Religion and Ethics – RST3A

Date: ....

Time: ....

Location: ....

A2 Philosophy of Religion – RST3B

Date: ....

Time: ....

Location: ....

A2 Religion and Human Experience – Topic I Life, death and beyond – RST4A

Date: ....

Time: ....

Location: ....

A2 Religion and Human Experience – Topic III Religious experience – RST4A

Date: ....

Time: ....

Location: ....

1 Libertarianism, free will and determinism

Key concepts

To what extent are human beings truly free? There are three positions to consider:

1 **Hard determinism** argues that every event has a cause or many causes and therefore the idea of freedom of the will is impossible. We only think that we have **free will** because we are not aware of all the causes of our actions.

2 **Soft determinism** or **compatibilism** argues that although we may be determined by some factors such as our genes and environment we can still function as free moral agents. This position proposes that true free will needs an element of **determinism** otherwise everything would be too random or down to chance.

3 **Libertarianism** argues that we cannot really establish any truth to determinism because our own experiences dictate that we make free choices. It is only this freedom that can make sense of moral responsibility. It is reason and the will that supersede the physical element of **causality** and belong to the **metaphysical** realm.

> **Free will** – the ability to make choices that are not determined by prior causes or by divine intervention.
>
> **Determinism** – for everything that happens there are conditions such that, given those conditions, nothing else could happen.
>
> **Causality** – the idea that one action or event gives rise to another in a collective series of events.
>
> **Metaphysical** – to do with a non-physical realm.

Free will

Free will is about having the individual freedom to decide one's destiny. Are we really responsible for our own choices in life or is there a causally dependent destiny for us that we cannot escape?

If we do not have freedom of choice, then how can we be to blame for our actions and the decisions that we make? This leads many thinkers to assume that if we blame or praise people for actions they freely and knowingly undertake, then it is vital for human beings to have freedom to act. The very basis of morality is dependent upon freedom. As Kant (1724–1804) suggested, if there is an 'ought' to our behaviour then there also needs to be a 'can do' to it. A moral obligation or duty implies that this is possible to exercise.

Question of genetics and environment (internal and external causations)

Revised ☐

Are we 'made' to behave the way we do because of our environment and upbringing, or do we have an essential genetic disposition that dictates our behaviour? This is often referred to as the 'nature or nurture' debate.

One famous example of this is the case of an American lawyer called Clarence Darrow who took on the case of Leopold and Loeb in Chicago in 1924. These teenage boys were accused of kidnapping and killing another teenager. Darrow argued that his clients were not completely responsible for their actions, but the products of the environment they grew up in. Indeed, they were influenced by the philosophy of Nietszche. Leopold had written to Loeb before the murder and quoted: 'A superman … is, on account of certain superior qualities inherent in him, exempted from the ordinary laws which govern men. He is not liable for anything he may do.'

Exam practice answers at **www.therevisionbutton.co.uk/myrevisionnotes**

Darrow argued 'this terrible crime was inherent in his organism, and it came from some ancestor ... Is any blame attached because somebody took Nietzsche's philosophy seriously and fashioned his life upon it? ... It is hardly fair to hang a 19-year-old boy for the philosophy that was taught him at the university'. Therefore, the boys were not fully responsible for their actions because they were determined by a mixture of their genetic disposition to be attracted to a particular philosophy and an education that influenced this destiny. Although guilty of a crime, they were not totally morally responsible for it. Using this argument, they were sentenced to life imprisonment rather than the death penalty.

There are therefore two very pertinent points to consider regarding free will.

1   The genetic aspect of our make-up. This argues that we inherit and pass on traits from our parents and this makes up the DNA of an individual. It is the same for moral freedom and behaviour as it is for our physical body in which genes are directly responsible for the way a person looks, their sex, hair colour, race and many other factors. These 'other factors' extend to the idea of behaviour or a genetic predisposition to act in a certain way. Our genetics mean we are 'programmed' just like a computer.

2   The extent to which our social context affects and controls our behaviour, and adds the extra features to this programming. Psychologists have long argued that our upbringing influences our actions.

Free will curtailed by volition

Revised ☐

There is, however, a problem with the nature or nurture debate. What happens when a person acts contrary to their upbringing or genetic disposition? Can this be demonstrated? Is this possible? The nature or nurture debate does not allow for the possibility of the strength of will power, restraint and self-discipline.

Aristotle recognised that there are different 'characters' – those who could exercise will power to different extents and those who could not. For Aristotle, this was the very basis of morality and moral responsibility. Some can resist temptations to act in a certain way while others cannot. How do we explain this?

Our legal system is built upon the understanding that our will and intention feature heavily in our actions. Likewise, the Indian concept of **karma** (action) is not just about 'action', but rather, as the Buddha argued, volition: 'Volition, O monks, is what I call karma, for through volition one performs the action'. Hence both the Buddhist philosophy and our legal system distinguish between three elements:

- premeditated action when someone is in complete control of their actions through will
- diminished responsibility when other factors, both external (environment) and internal (disposition), have dictated actions
- a lack of compunction whereby the agent is totally unaware of the moral consequences of their actions.

Moral freedom, for some, is about exercising will power and being in control of our actions so that we are responsible for our own lives.

> **Karma** – literally 'action' that a person does that is measured as morally significant.

> **Key quote**
>
> 'Karma, correctly speaking, denotes the wholesome and unwholesome volitions and their concomitant mental factors, causing rebirth and the destiny of beings.'
>
> (Nyanatiloka, Buddhist monk and scholar)

Contracting into societies
Revised

The extent to which we set the parameters for action and accept behavioural norms is another aspect to freedom, or the appearance of freedom. Society has a set of rules that are followed and this is sometimes referred to as a **social contract**. Accepting rules means that we limit our behaviour. This is the only way society can function justly and protect the freedom and rights of everyone involved. If there were no rules or acceptance of behavioural norms, then how could society function?

> **Social contract** – the unwritten agreement in society that a citizen agrees to in relation to following the rules that society sets.

Conflict of free wills
Revised

Another problem with the idea of total, unrestrained freedom is that wills can conflict. For example, if I am allowed free speech does this mean I am entitled to say anything in public no matter how malicious? If I have the freedom to move then can I just go anywhere? Obviously, there have to be restraints on our freedoms depending on the social context, for example, the law. Individual rights need to be exercised within the parameters of social contracts and any individual conflicts of freedoms must be dealt with. We are, in essence, allowed as much individual freedom as our social context affords us practically.

> **Exam tip**
>
> Make sure that you can use the technical vocabulary effectively and accurately when answering questions on free will.

> **Now test yourself**
> Tested
>
> 1 How is free will pertinent to the study of ethics?
> 2 State two ways in which free will may be an illusion.
> 3 Why is will power important for the idea of free will?
>
> **Answers on page 106**

Libertarianism

This is the idea that our lives are fully within our control in terms of moral behaviour. The libertarian Peter Van Inwagen (b. 1942) believes that free will is incompatible with determinism. He uses the analogy of a 'fork' in the road and argues that we consciously make choices in life to take paths that we wish to follow. This, then, is dependent upon the idea that choices are possible for us to make. If there were no choices then there would be no fork in the road and there would only be one response possible. This is sometimes called the consequence argument.

Our experience tells us that we do indeed make choices. Choices are available for us and these choices are within our own power to make. If we were completely determined by our genes and our environment then there could be no fork in the road. There would be no reason to stop and deliberate.

This has been criticised because it assumes that our lives are like roads and that movement in life is always forwards and indeed straightforward.

For the libertarian we have to be fully free or not free at all. The libertarian rejects the idea that we are determined by some things so that we appear to have choice. The libertarian argues that the compatibilist (soft determinist) presents a no-choice principle since their understanding of choice, in effect, is only the appearance of choice. In reality, it is no choice at all.

The position of the libertarian does depend upon the idea that we have a distinct personality or moral self that incorporates the conscience.

> **Key quote**
>
> 'Determinism (without these additional and controversial assumptions) does not have the consequence that our "journey" through life is like moving down a road; the contrast between determinism and non-determinism is not the contrast between travelling on a branching road and travelling on a road with no branches.'
>
> (Stanford Encyclopaedia of Philosophy)

The personality and the moral self

Revised

Human beings consist of both physical and mental properties. The idea that a human being has a personality reflects the idea that this interacting group of mental and physical phenomena exhibit certain character traits that make a person who they are. Personality, then, is very much an **empirical** concept. Personality is subject to causes and conditions that change and mould it. But how does a bad person become good when all they know and experience is negative?

> **Empirical** – anything that is to do with the human senses.

For people to be able to change there must be some operative ethical aspect to a human being that distinguishes between self-interest and altruistic behaviour, between duty and desire. Additionally, this aspect for a libertarian thinker must involve an element of autonomy of the will to allow this freedom. This element of decision-making is made by the 'moral self', separate from the personality, which allows for a causally undetermined choice. It is through will power that this moral self can overcome personality traits and the pressures of the empirical self in order to make a morally correct choice. The causally undetermined choice is the aspect of a human being that allows for moral responsibility and distinguishes human beings from lesser animals and makes them, according to certain traditions of thinking, unique.

The conscience

The conscience is, in effect, the moral self. However, conscience is used and understood in a verbal way rather than as an 'essence' that exists as a separate entity within us. Conscience acts; it performs a function. This function has been described in many ways:

- The Concise Oxford English Dictionary describes it as 'a person's moral sense of right and wrong'.
- Thomas Aquinas (1225–1274) referred to it as 'the voice of our true selves'.
- 'The inbuilt monitor of moral action of choice values.' (John Macquarrie (1919–2007))
- St Paul saw it as bearing witness to truth: 'Since they show that the requirements of the law are written on their hearts, their consciences also bearing witness.' (Romans 2:15)
- St Augustine (354–430) has a similar view to St Paul: 'men see the moral rules written in the book of light which is called truth'.
- The Anglican priest and theologian Joseph Butler (1692–1752) saw conscience as a principle: 'There is a principle of reflection in men by which they distinguish between approval and disapproval of their own actions … this principle in man … is conscience.'

For libertarians, it is clear whatever the definition, that the conscience enables the decision-making process to function based upon the belief that what we are choosing is 'right' or 'good'. The ability to make decisions according to conscience is part of what it means to be a human being.

For the religious, the conscience may be seen as the inner voice of God. Aquinas took this view; part of becoming our true selves is to discover, through reason, the natural law established by God and to follow this. For Aquinas, conscience also acted as a deterrent for evil acts.

Joseph Butler emphasised the alternative function of conscience, namely that it directs a human being towards loving others and away from selfish acts. In this way conscience can never be wrong. Butler says, 'Had it strength as it has right; had it power as it has manifest authority, it would absolutely govern the world'.

According to Cardinal Newman (1801–1890), despite being Roman Catholic and following the Pope's guidance, the conscience has the authority of superseding this due to the fact that it is given by God. He famously wrote: 'I toast the Pope but I toast conscience first'. Roman Catholic teaching follows suit and recognises the crucial role and function of conscience by allowing believers the freedom not to be forced against what their conscience tells them.

> **Key quote**
>
> 'All are bound to follow their conscience in every sphere of activity so that they may come to God, who is their last end. Therefore, the individual must not be forced to act against conscience nor be prevented from acting according to conscience, especially in religious matters.'
>
> (Vatican Council)

The causally undetermined choice

Revised

If one is a libertarian then it must follow that choices are not predetermined by causes, genetic or environmental, and that the ethical decision made is therefore a causally undetermined choice, i.e. one of absolute freedom.

Traditionally, this has been explained by the idea of **dualism**, that is, the body–soul divide. For example, René Descartes (1596–1650) believed that the 'mind' or 'soul' was distinct from the body and the physical world. If an entity is distinct from the world then its activity would not be subject to the laws of nature that govern physical events. The soul or mind would interact with the physical world through influencing the brain's activity, allowing free choice to take place. Free choice would not be random or down to chance and neither would it be determined or caused by the physical aspects of the world.

> **Dualism** – the philosophy of mind (or soul) and body as being two separate entities.

> **Exam tip**
>
> Quotations are very useful to illustrate or support a point. You can always paraphrase if you can't remember the exact quotation.

Now test yourself

Tested

4 According to some people, what evidence is there that we have free will?

5 What does the libertarian mean by free will?

6 What is the difference between the personality and the moral self?

Answers on page 106

> **Typical mistake**
>
> Some candidates make vague and inaccurate references to religious teachings when in reality there are very specific teachings to be found.

Determinism

The principle of causality

Revised

The world around us is very much a 'closed' or **holistic** phenomenon. Causality and the interaction of phenomena are scientific observations. For the materialistic philosopher, even the interaction between mind and body has a physical cause. Everything has to have an explanation, therefore so does the way in which we choose to act. Any decision made has a cause. If this is the case then it is illogical to speak of 'free' choice or will because it is clear from our observations that everything is determined by causality.

> **Holistic** – concerning something that deals with the 'whole' picture.

Hard determinism

Revised

Hard determinism takes the no-nonsense line that everything that occurs in the universe has a sufficient explanation through causes and conditions, that is, the scientific law of cause and effect. In other words, our actions, the ones we actually do, are the only ones that we can do. In effect, human freedom becomes an illusion. It is a mere interpretation of what is happening in our world. Moreover, it is essentially an ignorant view of what is going on. It takes a very **materialist** stance in that it explains everything by physical processes. The brain essentially generates our thought processes.

> **Key quote**
>
> 'It follows … about states of the brain as effects, as correlates and as causes, that on every occasion when we decide or choose, we can only decide or choose as in fact we do.'
>
> (Ted Honderich)

> **Materialist** – the philosophy that everything human can be explained in empirical terms.

Although it may appear that human beings are in control, this is in fact an illusion. The idea of 'free will' becomes a defence mechanism in order to make sense of things but this view is, according to the philosopher John Locke (1632–1704), as ignorant as the person who awakes in a locked room and decides to stay there. It appears to be a free decision, but in reality the person has no choice but to remain there as the room is locked.

The hard determinist view has major implications for morality because it implies that we cannot be responsible for our actions.

Explanations of our 'nature' have been put forward by thinkers in three ways:

1 Behavioural science (for example, B F Skinner) argues that we are mere products of social conditioning.
2 Psychology (for example, Freud) argues that our desires and choices are residues of previous experiences.
3 Biological science (for example, R Dawkins) argues that we are driven by a selfish gene which instinctively works towards survival.

Nevertheless, it is important that hard determinists can explain good moral choices. Richard Dawkins (b. 1941) suggests that we can transcend our selfish gene through co-operation and kindness to others, what he refers to as a 'lust to be nice'.

For thinkers such as Dawkins then, a sense of moral responsibility transpires, or more accurately, moral ability emerges from this 'lust to be nice'.

> **Key quote**
>
> 'It follows too that we are not responsible for our decisions, choices or actions, and, what is most fundamental, that we do not possess selves of a certain character.'
>
> (Ted Honderich)

> **Key quote**
>
> 'There is no reason why the influence of the genes cannot be reversed by other influences … in fact genes only determine behaviour in a statistical sense.'
>
> (Richard Dawkins)

Soft determinism
Revised ☐

This is the position that the world is conditioned by causality but, due to the random nature of this causality, there is a need for free will in order to make sense of the moral and social order. Soft determinists are sometimes called compatibilists as they see free will and determinism working together. We are not morally responsible for some actions, for example, when we are forced to do something under threat of violence. However, there are actions that clearly have free choice.

Compatibilists argue that human beings are both free and determined by background, genetics, education and the laws of nature. David Hume (1711–1776) is the classic example of a soft determinist. Freedom requires determinism in order to make sense of things, otherwise everything would be random with no explanation. Freedom involves the empowerment to act and thus control the desired effect.

Modern thinkers such as Robert Kane (b. 1938) and Peter Vardy (b. 1945) have supported soft determinism. They argue that true freedom may never be achieved because of the complexity of genetic and environmental influences on us; however, this does not mean that freedom is not possible at all.

> **Key quote**
>
> 'By liberty, then, we can only mean a power of acting or not acting, according to the determinations of the will; that is, if we choose to remain at rest we may; if we choose to move, we also may.'
>
> (David Hume)

> **Key quote**
>
> 'If I suffered from a compulsion neurosis, so that I got up and walked across the room, whether I wanted to or not … then I should not be acting freely. But if I do it now, I shall be acting freely … For it is not when my action has any cause at all, but only when it has a special sort of cause, that it is reckoned not to be free.'
>
> (A J Ayer)

Kant

The philosopher Kant has been linked with both libertarianism and soft determinism. For Kant it is essential that libertarian freedom is there to explain morality. However, he also accepted that we are influenced by other phenomenal factors. Kant's view of morality and free will is inherently linked to his idea that there is a transcendent element to human nature that is grounded in reason and he distinguished between the phenomenal realm and the noumenal realm. The noumenal realm is free from the dictations of the phenomenal realm and is therefore free.

Kant's theory supports the autonomy (independence) of the will (libertarianism) and is why he is sometimes associated with libertarianism. However, Kant sees his freedom as something that is very different from randomness, and as something wholly compatible with the laws of the universe. The philosopher Roger Scruton explains Kant's view: 'The free agent is seen to be distinguished, not by his lack of constraint, but by the peculiar nature of the restraint that governs him. He is restrained by reason, in its reception to the moral law.' In a sense, Kant is a compatibilist but not necessarily a soft determinist!

> **Key quote**
>
> 'Now even if one believes the action to be determined by these causes one nonetheless blames the agent … this blame is grounded on the law of reason, which regards reason as a cause that, regardless of all empirical conditions just named, could have and ought to have determined the conduct of the person to be other than it is.'
>
> (Immanuel Kant)

Summary of positions for free will

Libertarianism	Kant	Soft determinism	Determinism
Undetermined	Determined but noumenal self is separate	Determined and linked to/ interaction with...	Determined
Total freedom	Rise above/determined to use reason	Limited free will choices	No free will

> **Typical mistake**
>
> Candidates sometimes misunderstand the demands of AO1. It is impossible to include everything in an answer and some candidates are not selective enough and try to 'write all they know'.

> **Exam tip**
>
> Make sure that you time your answers correctly in an examination and do not spend too much time on one answer at the expense of another one. AO1 is all about the skill of being able to select the correct amount of relevant information.

> **Now test yourself**   Tested ☐
>
> 7   How did John Locke explain free will?
> 8   What evidence suggests we are determined but yet do have some free will?
>
> **Answers on page 106**

A religious perspective on libertarianism and determinism

How do we know that we have free will and are free to choose when God is almighty, has ultimate power and knows everything? In contrast, the idea that we have been given laws and the guidance to live life a certain way is linked clearly to the idea of reward and punishment, that is, moral responsibility. Does it therefore follow that human beings must be free?

Christianity
Revised

Christians have often disagreed about the role of free will. St Augustine, whose thought influenced much of later theology, maintained the absolute rule of God over human will. He suggests that God does this by creating an infinite store of motives and the correlating foreknowledge of those to which the will of each human being would freely consent.

According to Roman Catholic teaching, human beings cannot have total freedom due to their lack of knowledge of the whole; freedom is simply an elective power of the will through reason.

Martin Luther (1483–1546) believed that sin has so clouded the human mind that our free will is severely restricted and that only by grace can we turn to God. He frankly stated that free will is a fiction, as humanity is bound to helplessness and slavery.

John Calvin (1509–1564) proposed we are totally predestined. For Calvin, God's preordination destroys the idea of free will, since human beings can perform no good act unless God's grace decrees it, which it is impossible to resist. It is both illogical and blasphemous to speak of the human will 'co-operating' with God's grace, for this would imply that human beings could resist God. The will of God, according to Calvin, is the very necessity of things.

The views of both Luther and Calvin are heavily dependent on the interpretation of certain elements of the writings of St Paul, which for some Christians is an unbalanced interpretation. The basic criticism is that there must be some autonomy of the will, otherwise reward and punishment would be unjust and this would contradict God's attributes.

Key quote

'For he chose us in him before the creation of the world to be holy and blameless in his sight.'

(Ephesians 1:4)

Exam tip

Make sure you are clear about which religious tradition you are referring to in the examination and try to choose diverse examples.

Now test yourself

9 Why does religion appear to suggest that human beings need free will?

10 Explain the idea of predestination.

Answers on page 106

Tested

Typical mistake

When talking about free will within religion, make sure that you outline the religious responses mentioning specific individual contributions to the debate such as the views put forward by Augustine, Calvin and Luther.

Exam practice answers at **www.therevisionbutton.co.uk/myrevisionnotes**

Issues arising

This first question asks us to consider the popular debate between determinists and libertarian thinkers about what 'freedom' actually is and what we mean by using the term in relation to actions and choices.

How free are human actions and choices?

Revised

How far are human beings free to make choices? This issue is an assessment of the free will and determinism argument.

Free choices	No free choices
• The libertarian view of free will demands total freedom with no causality. • Giving in to temptation or resisting temptation suggests autonomy and our experience thus tells us that we do make choices. • Desires and wants suggest persuasion and the possibility of alternative decisions being made. • The fear of (divine and/or legal) retribution and judgement suggests freedom otherwise religion and the idea of God would not make sense. • Human freedom provides a solution to the problem of evil and suffering, for example, that God is not responsible. • Forced action suggests there is an alternative – free action.	• God's traditional attributes of **omnipotence** and **omniscience** restrict freedom or make freedom a total contradiction. • **Predestination** teachings of Luther and Calvin do not allow for the free will of libertarian thought. • The teaching of hard determinism (through genes, upbringing, values, etc.) will not allow human autonomy of the will. • When people are coerced or forced into doing something it suggests a lack of freedom and one cannot prove any other alternative is possible.

Omnipotence – the power to do anything; all-powerful. Some philosophers exclude the logically impossible.

Omniscience – the ability to know everything; all-knowing.

Predestination – the religious idea that God has planned everything for us and that we cannot digress from this plan.

Exam tip

Feel free to raise questions and challenge views when dealing with an issue for AO2.

Can you ever have true libertarianism unless you are in complete isolation? Does libertarianism require no influences to be truly free?

Revised

This evaluation considers the challenge to dualistic thinking that even if there is something separate from the physical, it could never exert influence on the world of causes.

Exam tip

Always reflect on what you have written in your answer before drawing a conclusion.

Complete isolation/no influence	Interaction/influence
● Total freedom must be separate from any causes and conditions – there must be complete autonomy of the will. ● The idea of a 'moral self' suggests the level of independence is absolute and free from influence. ● For a decision to be free and for religious ideas of reward and punishment to work, there must be a pure view of free will without any influence.	● A 'free' choice affects the cause of events and determines other events, so how can it be totally independent? ● Soft determinism theory allows for both interaction and independence of the will. ● Determinists argue that it is impossible to be totally free. ● 'Complete isolation' does not mean 'no influence'; rather it means separation, and so libertarian thinking is justified.

Typical mistake

Some candidates just list a few points without truly evaluating or commenting on them. This means that their conclusions often have no link to what they have written before.

If we are not free, can we be held responsible for our actions?

Revised

The materialistic view of causality implies that there can be no autonomy of the human will when it comes to decision-making. This controversy is often contended today.

Arguments for no moral responsibility	Arguments for moral responsibility
● 'Real' liberty should mean just that, including consequences. ● The teaching of hard determinists such as Ted Honderich means that we cannot be held morally responsible for our actions. ● Blame is 'subjective' and thus unjustified when actions are 'objective'.	● There is a need for punishment if our freedom of action causes harm to others. ● The idea of causation does not necessarily exclude freedom according to soft determinists. ● If we are aware of consequences then we can restrain our behaviour. ● If there is freedom there must be responsibility; freedom and responsibility go hand in hand.

Typical mistake

Candidates sometimes run out of time for the evaluation part of a question. Make sure you know the timings and mark allocation for each question, and plan your time accordingly.

Strengths and weaknesses of libertarianism, free will and determinism for making ethical choices

Throughout the chapter there have been summaries of the opposing positions of freedom and determinism. Some of the key strengths and weaknesses are considered here.

Libertarianism and free will

Strengths	Weaknesses
• Libertarianism recognises moral responsibility and this also encourages people to seek behaviour that is constructive and meaningful to society. • It explains the moral diversity of our world given the fact that different people will make different decisions. • The belief in free will justifies reward and punishment sanctions and 'makes sense' of things, justifying the parameters of our societies and legal systems.	• Libertarianism does not recognise the finding of science that everything is determined and interconnected. • Libertarianism does not allow for conditioning of behaviour when scientific experiments demonstrate that this occurs. • Libertarianism cannot explain why actions and behaviour are chaotic if uncaused. • Libertarianism has the problem that there is conflict when one person's liberty opposes the freedom of another person, meaning that no one can be said to have true liberty.

Determinism

Strengths	Weaknesses
• Moral responsibility is recognised in soft determinism. • It is in accordance with what we know from behavioural science. • It is in agreement with what we know from psychology. • It is in line with what we know from biology and genetics.	• Determinism is too inflexible a system to be true and is not always in accordance with what we actually experience. • Determinism cannot explain human nature and behaviour effectively enough. • Determinism denies all moral responsibility and this would be devastating for society.

Now test yourself

11 Suggest two arguments for human beings being totally free.

12 Suggest two arguments that challenge the idea of libertarianism.

Answers on page 106

Exam tip

When evaluating free will and determinism, try to explore the implications of each viewpoint by explaining what would be the consequence for religious teaching and practice.

Exam practice

(a) Explain the idea that human beings have free will. (30 marks)

(b) 'Modern science clearly demonstrates that the idea of free will is an illusion.' Assess this view. (20 marks)

Answers online

Online

Typical mistake

Candidates can sometimes present an unbalanced argument that does not do justice to the wider consideration of the issues arising.

2 Virtue ethics

Key concepts

With **virtue ethics** we see a clear shift away from identifying ethical theory as being found in 'rules' or 'principles' (deontology – for example, natural law) or in 'consequence' (teleology – for example, situation ethics), to the quality, correct manner or disposition (hexis) of a human being. Right or wrong are not a matter for rules. Virtue ethics is all about how an individual can develop the correct 'character' (ethos) so as to behave virtuously, and, accordingly, in a way that is morally correct.

> **Virtue ethics** – the theory that ethics is all to do with a person's specific moral virtues.

Aristotle's view

Happiness (eudaimonia)　　　　　　　　　　　　　　　　　Revised ☐

The Greek word **eudaimonia** is key to understanding virtue ethics. For Aristotle (384–322 BCE), the word meant happiness or well-being in the sense of being successful or fulfilled. However, it is not a disposition like a virtue but rather an activity of the virtuous person. Eudaimonia is the end product generated, the outcome of being virtuous.

The goal of virtue ethics, then, is to create the good life, to be happy and fulfilled through cultivating virtues (**arete**). It is sometimes known as aretaic ethics. Eudaimonia is integral to every virtuous thing that we do in life. Rather than it being some sort of abstract substance to tap into, 'happiness is an activity of the soul in accordance with virtue' (Roger Scruton); that is, it is more about 'doing' than 'being' and this is very significant as the optimum disposition for eudaimonia is in accordance with virtuous behaviour. The goal of virtue ethics is to cultivate a virtuous disposition that brings about eudaimonia through virtuous actions.

Virtue ethics is grounded in Aristotle's book *Nichomachean Ethics* (NE). However, the origins of virtue ethics tie in with Aristotle's whole view about the universe, the four causes and idea of teleology (an ultimate goal).

Eudaimonia, then, incorporates the idea of well-being, 'peace' and goodwill to all, but it also incorporates the physical good life. Aristotle's virtue ethics is a **holistic** philosophy that must have a social context and the end result of enabling people to live together.

Overall, there are three aspects to happiness according to Aristotle:

1　a life of enjoyment
2　a life with freedom
3　being a philosopher (a life of reflection and contemplation).

> **Eudaimonia** – a Greek word used by Aristotle to define the end purpose of human life to be happiness, flourishing or fulfilment.
>
> **Arete** – virtue.
>
> **Holistic** – concerning something that deals with the 'whole' picture.

Key quotes

'Every art and every inquiry, and similarly every action and pursuit, is thought to aim at some good; and for this reason the good has rightly been declared to be that at which all things aim.'

　(Aristotle, NE, Book 1, Chapter 1)

'Happiness means the general condition of fulfilment or "success". It is absurd to ask why we should pursue it, since success or fulfilment is what every activity intends.'

　　(Roger Scruton, philosopher)

'Happiness, then, is something final and self-sufficient, and is the end of action.'

　(Aristotle, NE, Book 1, Chapter 7)

Exam practice answers at **www.therevisionbutton.co.uk/myrevisionnotes**

The most important virtue of all, wisdom, is the overall characteristic of a person who can maintain all three. Such wisdom is not easily gained and the good life is not easily or quickly achieved. As Aristotle says, 'But we must add "in a complete life". For one swallow does not make a summer, nor does one day; and so too one day, or a short time, does not make a man blessed and happy' (NE, Book 1, Chapter 7).

Now test yourself

Tested

1 What does virtue ethics concern itself with?
2 Where can we find Aristotle's ideas about virtue ethics?

Answers on page 106

Exam tip

Do not answer a question by simply giving a descriptive account. Your answer should always select the key events, that is, the appropriate information relevant to the question. This demonstrates more personal understanding or 'ownership' of the knowledge. It is evidence that 'information is mostly accurate and relevant' (AO1).

Typical mistake

Make sure that you time your answers correctly and have enough time left to answer the whole of the question.

Moral and intellectual virtues

Revised

The Greek term arete means 'virtue' but it also conveys the meaning of moral excellence, intellectual excellence and also physical excellence. Virtue is the idea of being how we are meant to be or being 'fit for purpose'.

According to Aristotle, there are two kinds of virtue: moral and intellectual. The moral virtues are acquired through habit and developed through practice. In contrast, the intellectual virtues are developed by education.

The moral virtues as discussed by Aristotle are:

- courage
- temperance
- liberality
- generosity (munificence or magnificence)
- pride (high-mindedness, concerned with honour)
- right or proper ambition
- patience
- truthfulness
- wittiness
- friendliness
- modesty
- righteous indignation.

The intellectual virtues as discussed by Aristotle include:

- intelligence
- practical reason
- theoretical reason
- understanding and good, or common, sense.

However, the most important are wisdom and justice.

Once again, it is important to note that such virtues are not easily learned but rather cultivated carefully. Aristotle compares the development of such virtues with at first a 'sketch' that gradually develops into a picture.

Now test yourself

Tested

3 Explain how a moral virtue is different from an intellectual virtue.
4 Which are the two most important intellectual virtues?

Answers on page 106

Exam tip

Make sure that you know all about the virtues as outlined by Aristotle as Aristotle's theory is the basis of virtue ethics for any system that is discussed.

Key quotes

'Since happiness is an activity of soul in accordance with perfect virtue, we must consider the nature of virtue; for perhaps we shall thus see better the nature of happiness.'

(Aristotle, NE, Book 1, Chapter 13)

'Virtue too is distinguished into kinds in accordance with this difference; for we say that some of the virtues are intellectual and others moral, philosophic wisdom and understanding and practical wisdom being intellectual, liberality and temperance moral.'

(Aristotle, NE, Book 1, Chapter 13)

'Virtue, then, being of two kinds, intellectual and moral, intellectual virtue in the main owes both its birth and its growth to teaching (for which reason it requires experience and time), while moral virtue comes about as a result of habit, whence also its name (ethike) is one that is formed by a slight variation from the word ethos (habit).'

(Aristotle, NE, Book 2, Chapter 1)

Typical mistake

Do not assume that the examiner knows the meaning of any technical terms you use. Make sure you explain them clearly.

Aristotle's doctrine of the mean
Revised

Key quote

'Virtue, then, is a state of character concerned with choice, lying in a mean … Now it is a mean between two vices, that which depends on excess and that which depends on defect; and again it is a mean because the vices respectively fall short of or exceed what is right in both passions and actions, while virtue both finds and chooses that which is intermediate. Hence in respect of its substance and the definition which states its essence virtue is a mean, with regard to what is best and right an extreme.'

(Aristotle, NE, Book 2, Chapter 6)

For Aristotle, cultivating virtues was to balance the two extremes of excess and deficiency. This is often referred to as the 'doctrine of the mean' although some writers also give it the title of the 'golden mean'. Each extreme brought with it an associated vice. Balancing the virtues and achieving the mean is no easy feat: 'Hence also it is no easy task to be good. For in everything it is no easy task to find the middle' (NE, Book 2, Chapter 9).

Aristotle's doctrine of the mean produces three types of person:

1 the **sophron** who naturally lives in the mean without effort
2 the **enkrates** who is tempted but has strong enough will power to live in the mean
3 the **akrates** (a 'person without will or weak-willed person') who is weak and cannot live in the mean by overcoming temptation of the vices. Such a character, according to Aristotle, is said to be incontinent (akrasia).

Sophron – someone who naturally lives in the mean without effort.

Enkrates – someone who is tempted but can resist through self-restraint.

Akrates – the weak-willed person who is undisciplined or incontinent (akrasia).

Excess-associated vice	Mean (virtue)	Deficiency-associated vice
Rashness	Courage	Cowardice
Licentiousness	Temperance	Insensibility
Prodigality	Liberality	Illiberality
Vulgarity	Generosity	Pettiness
Vanity	Pride/high-mindedness	Humility
Over ambition	Proper ambition	Lack of ambition
Boastfulness	Truthfulness	Understatement
Irascibility	Patience	Lack of spirit
Buffoonery	Wittiness	Boorishness
Obsequiousness	Friendliness	Cantankerousness
Shyness/bashfulness	Modesty	Shamelessness
Envy/spitefulness	Righteous indignation	Malicious enjoyment/callousness

Cardinal virtues and capital vices
Revised

There are, according to Aristotle, four cardinal virtues: temperance (moderation) and courage (which are both moral virtues), together with justice and wisdom (which are both intellectual virtues). These virtues were seen to be the most important for a character to develop, with wisdom being the virtue that manages and drives them all.

Exam practice answers at **www.therevisionbutton.co.uk/myrevisionnotes**

With this idea of cardinal virtues there later developed within the early Christian tradition, and then later on with Thomas Aquinas, the idea of cardinal vices – pride, avarice, lust, envy, gluttony, sloth – also known as the seven deadly sins (or cardinal sins). However, this was very much a later development, as the historian W Reade points out: 'In one sense, neither Aristotle nor any other ancient philosopher can be said to authorize either the general notion of a capital vice or the special list accepted by St Thomas and so many other Christian writers' (W Reade, *The Moral System of Dante's Inferno*, Kessinger Publishing 2004, originally published 1909).

Nonetheless, the idea of the vices of deficiency and excess are Aristotle's and with these he developed the notion of different character (see above), of which the juxtaposition between the man of virtue and the incontinent man was key.

> **Exam tip**
>
> When discussing virtue ethics, do not simply list the virtues but be selective, using Aristotle's three characters to exemplify them.

> **Typical mistake**
>
> Some candidates confuse the virtues and the vices, especially since Aquinas lists pride as one of the seven sins.

Now test yourself   Tested ☐

5   List the two aspects of Aristotle's doctrine of the mean.

Answer on page 106

Modern virtue ethics

In her article entitled 'Modern Moral Philosophy' (*Philosophy*, vol. 33, no. 124, 1958), Elizabeth Anscombe was the first modern philosopher to return to analyse human qualities as a key to ethical theory. She rejected absolutist approaches because she saw them as requiring a God. For Anscombe, the only progress in ethics would be to pursue 'human flourishing' (eudaimonia).

Alasdair MacIntyre   Revised ☐

In his book *After Virtue* (University of Notre Dame Press, 1981), MacIntyre argued that meta-ethics had left us in a 'moral vacuum'. By this he meant that the study of ethics had been drawn away from its social and historical context and that although a modern approach to ethics was not quite abstract it did not have firm grounding to demonstrate how ethics had developed. He proposed a historical approach to ethics – its 'narrative context' – that reflected an awareness of how ethics had developed which then tells us much about what it now is.

MacIntyre rejected what he called 'quandary ethics', which were discussions about ethics based upon unrealistic dilemmas. Instead, the focus should be on a specific situation for which ethics helps us to understand 'what sort of person I need to be'. Neither is ethics about abstractly selecting and applying rules meaninglessly. He argued that virtues can change in terms of their importance and usefulness for society because we value different things as people – ethics is about appreciating the social and historical contexts within which ethical dilemmas arise. Greek heroes, for example, were defined by their actions, virtues and vices. MacIntyre saw the key to Aristotle's theory was that the virtues such as truthfulness, courage and justice were essential virtues to maintain not only a good, moral character but also the integrity of a community.

> **Key quote**
>
> 'The list of virtues in the Ethics is not a list resting on Aristotle's own personal choices and evaluations. It reflects what Aristotle takes to be "the code of gentlemen" in contemporary Greek Society. Aristotle himself endorses this code.'
>
> (Alasdair MacIntyre, *A Short History of Ethics,* Routledge, 2002)

MacIntyre developed Aristotle's virtues through the concepts of internal and external 'goods' and the idea of human beings as practical reasoners to create a narrative for a 'good' life. Internal goods were those actions that were obvious and direct, such as giving money to the poor. External goods were those that were produced 'out of' the moral act, for example, inspiring others to behave morally. He also described three archetypal characters (bureaucratic manager, rich aesthete, therapist) that had come to dominate the ethos of modern society, all of which obscure true virtue. The characteristics of these characters are that they use people, money or materialism as ways of manipulating others for their own self-interest. For MacIntyre, the ideal 'character' as a role model for modern society is the philosopher.

Philippa Foot
Revised

Another important philosopher of modern times to champion virtue ethics was Philippa Foot (1920–2010). In her work *Virtues and Vices* (Blackwell, 1978) she argued that although aretaic ethics does not guarantee happiness, it is often a part of achieving it. Foot was one of the founders of Oxfam and firmly believed that ethics is about improving the world for others, both for individuals and for communities. She compared virtue ethics to navigation away and through obstacles, a bit like charting a course at sea.

The main differences between Foot and Aristotle are:

- according to Foot, wisdom is both a moral virtue and an intellectual virtue
- according to Foot, anyone can achieve wisdom as it does not rely on social status, political power or intellectual power
- Foot developed Aristotle's idea of the sophron by distinguishing between the moral hero (one who does good but whose intentions may not be pure) and the moral saint (one who does good and whose intentions are pure).

Foot rejects pride as a virtue in the way Christian tradition did (later identified by Aquinas as a vice) although there is debate about what Aristotle meant by the virtue pride with some arguing that it is more a justified and realistic self-esteem than an egotistical tendency. In other words, there is a difference between the person who thinks they are great and the one who actually knows greatness because they are great. It is not boastfulness, according to Aristotle, just an awareness of who they are.

Key quote

'Virtue is not, like a skill or an art, a mere capacity; it must actually engage the will.'

(Philippa Foot)

Key quote

'It is primarily by his intentions that a man's moral dispositions are judged.'

(Philippa Foot)

Exam tip

When discussing virtue ethics make sure that you compare and contrast the different theories rather than just stating what they are.

Typical mistake

It is not enough to say that MacIntyre and Foot developed Aristotle's theory; for high marks you have to demonstrate how.

Now test yourself
Tested

6 Explain why MacIntyre believed the study of meta-ethics had left a 'moral vacuum'.
7 Identify MacIntyre's three archetypal characters of the modern world.
8 State two differences between Foot and Aristotle.

Answers on page 106

Application to an ethical issue

The use of wealth

The best moral issue for virtue ethics to deal with is probably one that Aristotle deals with himself in *Nichomachean Ethics* – the use of wealth. Aristotle's approach to ethics is grounded in virtue, and how one responds to the materialistic context is crucial in developing such virtue. The two significant virtues for dealing with the use of wealth are liberality and magnificence. The development and adoption of such virtues by peoples and governments around the world would have massive implications for world poverty and suffering.

Several factors are important in dealing with wealth and addressing poverty in the modern world according to virtue ethics:

● Governments and individuals have to be generous but their actions must not be tainted with the vices of meanness or wastefulness.

● This response to the issue is once again seen as a balancing act between extremes of vices – for example, the famous response of Christian Aid to world poverty can be found in the quote 'give a man a fish and you feed him for a day, teach a man to fish and you feed him for life'.

● The ideal is to balance needs through the highest virtue of wisdom by considering the point at which human aid shifts from allowing dependence (short-term emergency aid) to independence (long-term aid strategies to help people survive in the future).

● At the heart of this example is Aristotle's principle to use money freely but wisely.

● To allow total dependence would be wasteful of resources; to ignore poverty would be mean.

● To encourage independence as well as providing immediate short-term aid is the action of a virtuous person or government.

Exam tip

Although you may have studied the application of virtue ethics to one moral issue, it may be an advantage for AO2 to look at other applications for wider consideration and evaluation.

Typical mistake

Candidates often explain the ethical theory in detail but forget to illustrate it with appropriate applications and examples.

Key quote

'With regard to giving and taking of money the mean is liberality, the excess and the defect prodigality and meanness. In these actions people exceed and fall short in contrary ways; the prodigal exceeds in spending and falls short in taking, while the mean man exceeds in taking and falls short in spending … With regard to money there are also other dispositions – a mean, magnificence (for the magnificent man differs from the liberal man; the former deals with large sums, the latter with small ones), an excess, tastelessness and vulgarity, and a deficiency, niggardliness; these differ from the states opposed to liberality, and the mode of their difference will be stated later.'

(Aristotle, NE, Book 2, Chapter 7)

Now test yourself

9 Why is the use of wealth a good moral issue to apply to virtue ethics?

10 State the two virtues relevant to the use of wealth.

Answers on page 106

Tested

Issues arising

Strengths and weaknesses of virtue ethics as an ethical system

Revised ☐

It is important to consider both the advantages and the possible shortfalls, or practical problems, of adopting a virtue ethics approach in relation to the modern world.

Weaknesses	Strengths
● It has been argued that virtue ethics is self-centred, for example, the idea of well-being can be understood as self-interest or, at the very least, has the potential for this. ● As a system, virtue ethics can be argued to be arbitrary, imprecise and vague because it lacks a focus on real behaviour in relation to real-life situations. More guidance is required. ● As a system, virtue ethics can be contradictory. If there are differences in expressing a virtue then which is the right one to choose? It is very subjective. ● It is too individualistic because it deals primarily with the individual. ● It is too intellectual for the simple human being; even Aristotle recognised that not everyone has the same ability when resisting vice. ● In virtue ethics there is too much dependence on the potential goodness of others. It is almost naïve, with no quality control. ● Virtue ethics can be seen to exhibit **speciesism** with its focus on humanity as the supreme being. Philosophers like Peter Singer would take issue with this.	● The virtues are self-focused but are in fact 'other regarding'. Although virtue ethics begins with the self it then moves on to develop a character that responds best to others and hence builds an ideal community. ● There is a social context for virtue ethics and in this way it is a very practical system. It focuses on the way we behave and not simply what we believe should be the case! ● The virtuous person is an 'exemplar' and therefore it has clear guiding principles. It also acknowledges the fact that such exemplars (philosophers) can serve as good role models. ● The wisdom in application and the delivery of justice for society ensure that it works and is not subjective. ● Virtue ethics appeals to feminist thinkers as an alternative to rules/duties which, some argue, is a stereotypically male way of approaching life. Most of the systems in place have been devised by men for men. ● Virtue ethics is a **naturalistic** system and not dependent on religion. ● Virtue ethics enables people to learn to become moral and promotes change that will last.

Naturalistic – a system that can be explained in a natural as opposed to a supernatural way.

Speciesism – the belief that human beings are better than other species.

Exam tip

For AO2 answers, demonstrate that you are using evaluation skills by establishing a clear process of reasoning in your answer. Raising your own questions is a good way of enhancing this.

Is virtue ethics really different from deontological and teleological systems?

Revised

The issue with virtue ethics as a system is that it does not conveniently fall within the 'deontological' or **'teleological'** category due to its focus on the characteristics of a person. Nonetheless, its links with Aristotle and Aquinas have caused some to question whether or not it is really a form of natural law. Others see it as more 'teleological' due to its focus on achieving eudaimonia.

> **Teleological** – concerning the idea that there is a purpose to some thing or action that can be seen by looking at the outcome or end.

These are some of the points that may be raised:

Same	Different
• In virtue ethics there is some idea of 'duty' and 'doing the right thing' and it is this aspect that makes it similar to deontological approaches such as natural law or Kantian ethics. • The question could be asked, 'Are the virtues really moral absolutes?' and, if so, are they similar to deontology? • The theory of virtue ethics can be compared to Kant's ideas of imperatives and universalism. • Some thinkers, for example, Mel Thompson, see it as merely an extension of natural law. • Due to the fact that virtue ethics sees every moral dilemma as contextual it is therefore very similar to teleological theories such as utilitarianism and, especially, situation ethics.	• Virtue ethics is clearly person-centred, which makes it very different from a focus on rules, a consideration of the outcome or even the use of an ultimate guiding principle. • The virtues found within virtue ethics are clearly different to any kind of rules or principles found in deontological or teleological theories. • Some would argue that as it is seen as a departure from natural law, it is therefore not the same! A common basis does not necessitate a common outcome.

> **Typical mistake**
>
> Candidates sometimes get their technical and religious terminology confused.

The significance of a particular view of human nature for virtue ethics

Revised

The very basis of virtue ethics assumes a range of things about what it means to be human. In your lessons you should have debated some of these key questions, some of which are listed below. For each question, try to think of a clear example that would support your argument.

Key questions include:

- Do virtues really exist? For example, there are various degrees of behaviour and there have been clear instances in the history of the world when one society's virtue is considered another society's vice.

- In addition, if the virtues are real, do human beings really want to develop such virtues? For example, if everyone insisted that the other should enter the door before them, no one would ever get through!

- Does virtue ethics provide sufficient insight into human nature to be used effectively? For example, we have already seen that there are different views about Aristotle's understanding of what 'pride' is.

- Is virtuous action really driven by self-interest? For example, am I being virtuous because the reward is being virtuous or because being virtuous brings a reward? Do I want another person to be first so that in being last I will inevitably be first in terms of virtue? Or, do I go first knowing that another will, by virtue of being last, become first ... then in knowing this do I become first? The questions are unanswerable.

- Is it really a possibility for anyone to achieve the highest virtues of character?

> **Exam tip**
>
> Ensure that you can demonstrate your knowledge of the different views as this is especially relevant for AO2 when moving from considering one position to another.

How compatible is virtue ethics with a religious approach to ethics?

One of the crucial issues of any ethical system for Religious Studies is how that system relates to the ethical approaches found within religion today. It is this compatibility or incompatibility that will determine how people of faith from around the world respond to virtue ethics.

Compatible	Incompatible
• One of the great strengths of virtue ethics is that it stresses altruism, that is, a concern for the well-being of others. This is a teaching consistent with all forms of religion. • Virtue ethics also promotes the responsibility of the individual to better themselves, which is another feature of religious teaching. • If virtue ethics were not compatible with religion then people such as Aquinas would not have developed the theory.	• The problem with having no rules to follow is that it could encourage an 'anything goes' society, which is certainly not consistent with religion. • The liberal and relative aspect to virtue ethics means that it will not appeal to more conservative, traditional religious followers. • The focus on the individual together with some of the other weaknesses listed above would make it unattractive to religious believers. • The final point to consider is that there are other ethical systems that are more attractive and compatible for the religious believer, such as utilitarianism and situation ethics.

Now test yourself

11 List two strengths of virtue ethics.

12 List two weaknesses of virtue ethics.

Answers on page 106

Exam practice

(a) Examine one theory of virtue ethics and apply it to any ethical issue apart from science and technology. **(30 marks)**

(b) 'Virtue ethics has too many weaknesses to be taken seriously as an ethical approach to the problems of the modern world.' Assess this view. **(20 marks)**

Answers online

Online

Exam tip

Remember that for an AO2 answer you should be prepared to mix and match your thoughts on each particular area. For example, questions as to the strengths and weaknesses are relevant to other issues arising.

3 Religious views on sexual behaviour and human relationships

Different views on marriage

Key quote

'Marriage may be a useful tool of the state to regularise relationships, to protect children and administer rights of property, but since many people today consider living together or cohabitation as a natural way to express themselves sexually, the moral reasons for marriage may appear obscure and old-fashioned.'

(Michael Wilcockson)

Scripture-based ideas
Revised

The Bible teaches marriage as a good way of life. There are many examples of this teaching throughout both the Old and New Testaments. There are, however, no details of wedding ceremonies given within the Bible.

Although Genesis seems to condone **polygamy** and the use of concubines for reproduction, this is seen to be a contextual matter socially and is not pursued as an ideal, although the Mormon Church today still allows polygamy.

Polyandry is not really a feature of Christianity, the Bible or of any Hebrew culture. The closest to this is when a woman has a relationship outside of marriage but this is technically superseded by the sin of adultery.

Key quote

'For this reason a man will leave his father and mother and be united to his wife, and they will become one flesh.'

(Genesis 2:24)

Polygamy – a man having more than one wife.

Polyandry – a woman having more than one husband.

Institutional-based ideas: teachings from the Christian Church
Revised

Church of England clergy are obliged to marry people if at least one of them belongs to their parish, even if they are not practising Christians. For a ceremony outside a person's parish, special permission needs to be granted.

Marriage is a gift from God. It is one of the **sacraments** in Roman Catholicism and is for the purpose of procreation, a **covenant** in Protestantism and a mystical union in the Anglican Church. The Bible teaches marriage as a good way of life – the family unit promotes social stability.

Marriage is a demonstration of love and is for companionship. The procreation of children is seen to be a way of completing this union. Marriage avoids **illegitimacy**, it channels sexual instinct into a healthy relationship and gives it meaning.

Sacrament – a religious ceremony or sacred event in which God is believed to be present and an active participant.

Covenant – an agreement between God and human beings.

Illegitimacy – general term used mainly in the past to describe the state of children who are born outside marriage.

The importance of the institution of marriage can be seen from the ceremony and its symbolic representations. The vows in marriage have an emphasis on marriage for life ('until death') and also faithfulness ('to love and cherish … in sickness … until death'). The ceremony usually features several of the following:

- The bride wears white as a symbol of chastity.
- The vicar advises the congregation as to the purpose of the gathering, in the presence of God.
- Before the couple takes the vows, they and the congregation are asked if there is any reason why they should not be lawfully married.
- The bride and groom exchange vows that are spoken before God.
- The marriage is affirmed in the statement: 'That which God has joined together let no one separate'.
- Hymns and a brief sermon about love underline the seriousness of marriage.
- Sometimes the Eucharist is celebrated.
- Usually a meal of celebration follows.

Individual-based ideas   Revised ☐

It is now common, given the changing nature of relationships, family and ideas about marriage, to have individual practising Christians opt to live together and see the bonds of marriage as more spiritual than legal. Such Christians would argue that they do not need **secular** recognition of their relationship.

Likewise, there are people who are non-practising Christians who make their vows before God in church. Some Christian churches may ask that such a couple attend a course to understand the Christian faith before they get married.

Regarding remarriage, the Roman Catholic Church does not recognise divorce and the Pope has to **annul** a marriage. The Church of England allows its ministers to decide for themselves whether or not they will allow a remarriage ceremony to take place, with some only allowing an official 'blessing'.

> **Secular** – non-religious.
>
> **Annul** – to declare a marriage void; an act the Pope, the only person who can void a marriage, makes.

Now test yourself   Tested ☐

1 Outline one Scripture-based belief about marriage.
2 Outline two different institutional-based beliefs about the purpose of marriage.

Answers on page 106

> **Typical mistake**
>
> Candidates sometimes get specific teachings from different groups within a religion confused.

Sexual behaviour outside marriage

Age of consent, pre-marital sex, promiscuity and adultery

Revised ☐

In the United Kingdom, the age of consent to any form of sexual activity is sixteen for both men and women. The Sexual Offences Act of 2003 produced a series of laws intended to protect children under sixteen from sexual abuse. The Acts did not intend to prosecute mutually agreed teenage sexual activity, unless it involved abuse or exploitation.

Key quotes

'The term "pre-marital sex" can be understood in two ways. It can mean either indiscriminate sexual activity before a person settles to one partner in marriage, or the sexual expression of the love existing between two people who intend to marry (or who are in a long-term relationship).'

(Trevor Shannon)

'Increasingly, people claim that they embark on a sexual relationship as part of the quest for personal fulfillment … Sex is seen in that context – as a pleasure in itself, but also as a way of becoming intimate with the partner, sharing in a way that has an effect on the relationship as a whole.'

(Mel Thompson)

Although not illegal, adultery is still seen by society as a grave betrayal of trust in a relationship and it is the main reason for divorce proceedings to be fast-tracked. Additionally, sexual **promiscuity** is seen to be irresponsible due to the rise in teenage pregnancies and the fact that much promiscuity occurs under the influence of alcohol or drugs.

Pre-marital sex is not against the law and there are many people in society who engage in sexual activity within a long-term or serious loving relationship – secular monogamy. In general, this is seen as socially acceptable.

> **Promiscuity** – regular sexual activity with numerous partners outside the confines of a committed relationship.

Scripture-based ideas

Revised ☐

Jesus states that adultery is wrong and that it is the only reason for divorce. The universal acceptance of this within Christianity is reflected by one of the Ten Commandments: 'You shall not commit adultery' (Exodus 20:14).

Paul reminds believers that 'your body is a temple of the Holy Spirit' (1 Corinthians 6:19) and suggests that if a person is 'aflame with passion' then it is better to be married. Ultimately, the Bible teaches that sexual activity outside marriage is to be avoided.

Key quotes

'It is God's will that you should be sanctified: that you should avoid sexual immorality.'

(1 Thessalonians 4:3)

'But I tell you that anyone who divorces his wife, except for marital unfaithfulness causes her to become an adulteress.'

(Matthew 5:32)

Institutional-based ideas: teachings from the Christian Church

The traditional Christian teaching is that sex should be valued and given dignity within family life or a loving relationship. Roman Catholic teaching states that sex has both a unitive and procreative function. **Humana Vitae** teaches that these functions are inseparable. Family planning is acceptable but only through natural means.

The view of the Church of England is that sex depends upon the quality of the relationship and that it is reasonable to accept sexual relations as long as there is trust and commitment, respect and consent. Despite their differences, both denominations officially agree that sex outside matrimony, involving adultery, is wrong. However, official institutional declarations do not mean that individual Christians cannot follow their conscience.

Due to the sacred nature of marriage and the unchristian practice of deceit and dishonesty, adultery is frowned upon. However, forgiveness and reconciliation is often sought before considering divorce.

> **Humana Vitae** – paper written by Pope Paul VI in 1968 outlining Roman Catholic teaching on sexual matters and relationships.

Individual-based ideas

Christianity teaches that sex is an expression of love and responsibility. A sexual relationship reflects trust, respect and commitment. From the Christian perspective, it is generally regarded that sex, used wrongly, can encourage promiscuity, illegitimacy, moral disorder, adultery and a lack of trust in relationships. One of the main reasons for the ideal of sex *within* marriage is to protect individuals from the potential misuse and abuse of sex.

Some Christians would argue that while the principles of marriage are religious, marriage is also a social convention and a legal, secular contract. Therefore, as long as Christian principles are followed, sexual relationships outside of the legal contract of marriage but encompassing the Christian principles behind marriage, avoiding adultery and within the confines of the law, are acceptable. For example, a couple who love each other deeply are not breaking the law when they live together and are also encompassing the Christian principles behind marriage even though they are legally 'single'.

In addition to this, there are also those who do not choose to act in a sexual way, for example, nuns and monks. This is called abstinence.

> **Exam tip**
>
> It is vital to learn the key terms used for a topic. Accuracy is needed for the highest levels of understanding according to the level descriptors. Therefore it is important not to confuse the terms. Remember a few used correctly is far better than many used inaccurately.

> **Typical mistake**
>
> Don't use a quotation just for the sake of using a quotation – make sure that it is relevant to your answer.

> **Now test yourself**
>
> Tested
>
> 3 Outline two Scripture-based beliefs about sexual behaviour outside of marriage.
> 4 Give two different individual views on sexual behaviour outside of marriage to show how they can differ within Christianity.
>
> Answers on page 106

Human relationships

> **Key quote**
>
> 'It is true that for many societies and for much of history the legitimate expression of sexuality has been controlled by social norms, including the stability of family life … the prohibition of homosexuality, and the use of marriage as a means of forging political, financial or social links between families or even nations.'
>
> (Mel Thompson)

The abuse of power

Revised

It has often been said that sexual ethics is an issue of power, male dominance and oppression. The rights of women have long been lamented in our history. The restrictive use of marriage as a trading tool, bribe or resolution to a family conflict is all too familiar.

Historically, it is only relatively recently that the rights and freedoms of individuals have justly been addressed concerning issues of sexual equality. There have been long-awaited changes in laws, and changes in attitudes and moralities, reflected in the thinking of groups such as those advocating gay rights and **civil partnerships**.

> **Civil partnership** – a legal contract recognising the union of a couple who belong to the same sex.

> **Key quotes**
>
> 'The controversial philosopher Michel Foucault (1926–1984) even argued that the idea of "sexuality" is a modern invention designed to exercise political power over different members of society.'
>
> (Michael Wilcockson)
>
> 'Queer theory suggests that there can be no hard and fast boundaries about what is or is not a legitimate sexual relationship and no institution has the right to impose its views on others; being queer is the freedom to define oneself according to one's nature, whatever that may be.'
>
> (Michael Wilcockson)

Respect and responsibility: the role of men and women

Revised

Scripture-based ideas

The Bible outlines specific roles for men and women. Men must support their wives and families. Women must raise children and be homemakers. However, Galatians 3:28 clearly states that men and women are equals: 'There is neither … male nor female, for you are all one in Christ Jesus'. There are also examples of strong and respected women from the Old Testament – Ruth, Esther – which show how women have been regarded. Despite the Scriptural precedent for traditional distinctions, Christianity stresses that both roles are of equal status and importance.

Despite this there are some areas of the Bible where the approach and attitude towards women can be seen to be quite negative. St Paul taught that women were to be silent in church, cover their hair and be submissive to husbands. Furthermore, there have been several feminist responses to the Bible that point out its historical limitations and **patriarchal** bias, as well as issues of translation.

> **Patriarchal** – a word used to denote a male-dominated perspective.

Institutional-based ideas: teachings from the Christian Church

There are many different attitudes within Christianity on the roles of men and women. However, the main two are Protestant (Church of England) and Roman Catholic. Women are not allowed to become priests within the Catholic tradition. This is because Jesus' apostles were all male and Catholics want to maintain this tradition. Letters from St Paul support this stance, for example, 'I do not permit a woman to teach or to have authority over a man; she must be silent [in a place of worship]' (1 Timothy 2:12). St Paul also wrote 'The man is the head of the woman, as Christ is the head of the church'. Therefore if a Christian is part of the Catholic tradition, then they will have a more traditional view of the role of women.

However, the Church of England has a slightly more liberal view and has allowed women to become priests since 1994. As well as this, it tries to follow the example of Jesus, who had quite a modern view on the role of women for his time. An example of this is Jesus keeping women as companions – for example, his friendship with Mary and Martha. Women were also the earliest witnesses to his **resurrection**. Nonetheless, women are still not allowed to hold the position of bishop within the Church of England despite a recent vote by the Synod (although the view is that it is to be discussed again at a later stage).

There is, however, in both traditions the universal idea that 'breadwinning' is for men and raising children is for women. Ultimately, the attitudes to the role of men and women are dependent upon which Christian tradition is followed.

> **Resurrection** – coming back to life from the dead.

Individual-based ideas

Many Christian women work full-time or are the traditional 'breadwinner' in a relationship. Likewise, some Christian men have a more traditionally feminine role and take more responsibility for the family. Within most denominations throughout Christianity, the role of men and women within personal life is left to the individuals. Regarding the ceremonial aspects of the religion, the individual ideas of who takes what role are very much at the mercy of the teachings of the individual denomination.

Now test yourself   Tested ☐

5 Outline two Scripture-based beliefs about the roles of men and women.

6 Outline two different institutional-based beliefs about the role of men and women.

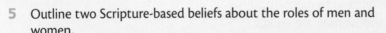

Answers on page 106

Some see homosexuality as a 'condition', others have argued that it is socially induced and some have even tried to establish that it is genetic. If we were to take the line of Foucault (see key quote from Michael Wilcockson on page 33), then it is interesting to see that the questions concerning homosexuality are no more relevant than those we could ask of any other sexual orientation. Indeed, why does there have to be a specific reason?

Considering that homosexuality has existed as far back in history as we can delve, it is surprising that the laws regarding the treatment of homosexuals and their rights have only been liberalised in the Western legal system relatively recently. Since this breakthrough in public and government acknowledgement of the rights of homosexuals, there have been several developments in the law:

- 1967: the age of consent for homosexual males was set at 21.
- 1994: the Criminal Justice and Public Order Act reduced the age of consent to 18.
- 2000: the Parliament Act was invoked to ensure the passage of the Sexual Offences (Amendment) Act 2000, which made the age of consent 16 for both homosexuals and heterosexuals.
- 2003: the Sexual Offences Act completely overhauled the outdated procedures for dealing with sexual offences, including making gross indecency, buggery and sexual activity between more than two men no longer crimes in the United Kingdom.

Indeed, as we write this book the coalition government is considering a redefinition of marriage so as to include two people of the same sex.

Scripture-based ideas

The writers of the Bible did not deal with the issue of homosexuality in a reasoned manner through dialogue and exploration of thought. It was not their intention to approach the subject in this way. There are only a few statements that are set in an historical context, for example, the views of a tribal culture found in the Old Testament: 'If a man lies with a man as one lies with a woman, both of them have done what is detestable. They must be put to death; their blood will be on their own heads' (Leviticus 20:13).

Alternatively, there is the promotion of the natural law ideal of heterosexual partnership: 'For this reason a man will leave his father and mother and be united to his wife, and they will become one flesh' (Genesis 2:24).

The New Testament, likewise, condemns homosexual activity, for example, the writings of St Paul: 'In the same way the men also abandoned natural relations with women and were inflamed with lust for one another. Men committed indecent acts with other men, and received in themselves the due penalty for their perversion' (Romans 1:27).

Key quote

'It is important to understand the distinction between homosexuality and homosexual acts. The condition of homosexuality means that a person, whether a man or a woman, is sexually attracted to persons of the same sex. The exact causes of this are unknown: they may be social, genetic or hormonal but the recognition of its existence is quite recent.'

(Trevor Shannon)

Key quote

'… it is pointless condemning someone for being homosexual: it is a condition that is not arrived at by choice … the homosexual, whether he or she indulges in homosexual acts or not, is a person loved by God and for whom Christ died.'

(Trevor Shannon)

Whatever the case, it is widely recognised that simply taking extracts from Scripture out of context and applying them to the modern context is not a legitimate way to interpret Scripture. It is interesting to note that some passages suggest strong male relationships, for example, the relationship between David and Jonathan whom David loved 'more than a woman' (2 Samuel 1:26), and strong female relationships, such as that of Ruth and Naomi.

Institutional-based ideas: teachings from the Christian Church

There is no doubt that homosexuality is a divisive issue in Christianity. Parts of the Christian tradition seem to be more open to embracing homosexuality as an acceptable lifestyle, whilst other parts of the Christian tradition remain very opposed and see it as against that which God intended. The religion encompasses all views and even has openly homosexual clergy, including bishops. The Church was divided by the appointment of its first openly gay bishop, Gene Robinson, in 2003.

Under Church of England guidance, gay clergy can enter a civil partnership if they provide reassurance that they will abstain from sex. Gay couples who ask a priest to bless their union must be dealt with 'pastorally and sensitively' on an individual basis.

> **Celibate** – to abstain from sexual relations, usually through personal choice or a vow.

Anglican bishops hold widely varying views on sexuality, due to the ambiguity in interpreting ancient passages from the Bible.

The Roman Catholic tradition recognises different sexual orientations but takes the Biblical line that homosexual acts are not 'natural' as God intended. This teaching is heavily influenced by the theory of natural law. Priests are **celibate** and so the issue of homosexual activity such as a long-term relationship does not affect the priesthood.

> **Exam tip**
>
> Make sure that for each issue you are aware of the difference between scripture-based ideas and those of an institution.

Individual-based ideas

As with marriage, the issue of homosexual activity is very much up to the individual. The Christian tradition is gradually becoming more tolerant and open. Some prejudice, however, still remains.

> **Typical mistake**
>
> Candidates sometimes mistakenly believe the views of an authoritative individual to be representative of either an institution or what the religious text may say.

> **Now test yourself**   Tested ☐
>
> 7 Outline two Scripture-based beliefs about homosexuality.
> 8 Outline two different institutional-based beliefs about homosexuality.
>
> Answers on page 106

Concept of love, family and children

Love
Revised ☐

The aspects of love have been categorised into four types: erotic love (**eros**), friendship love (**philia**), family love (**storge**) and lastly, a deep sense of true, pure love (**agape**) that St Paul uses in the New Testament, often translated as 'Christian love' or 'unconditional love'. The first three types feature in most relationships, but are surpassed by the universal fourth aspect, agape.

> **Eros** – sensual love.
> **Philia** – friendship love.
> **Storge** – family love.
> **Agape** – unconditional love or 'pure' love.

Scripture-based ideas

The Old Testament is written in Hebrew and the word used for the loving relationship between God and his people is 'hesed'. This describes a 'love' that is faithful, strong and kind, is often translated as 'loving kindness' or 'steadfast love' and incorporates the ideal of commitment. The Hebrew people were often reminded to consider or remember ('zochair') this love of God in terms of the action it produced in history when God intervened on their behalf, for example, the Exodus.

In the New Testament we have Jesus' example of sacrificial love and his teaching about the greatest commandment to 'love God and your neighbour as yourself'. Jesus' greatest actions were ones of sacrifice and unconditional giving. St Paul famously speaks of Christian love ('agape') in 1 Corinthians 13.

> **Key quote**
>
> 'Love is patient, love is kind. It does not envy, it does not boast, it is not proud. It is not rude, it is not self-seeking, it is not easily angered, it keeps no record of wrongs. Love does not delight in evil but rejoices with the truth. It always protects, always trusts, always hopes, always perseveres.'
>
> (1 Corinthians 13:4–7)

Institutional-based ideas: teachings from the Christian Church

The Christian Church has always advocated 'love' for fellow humanity in all its teachings and has a record of pastoral ministry to the wider community. There are many specific examples of missionary work that can be drawn upon.

Individual-based ideas

The American minister Joseph Fletcher based his whole theory of situation ethics around the concept of Christian love. However, the application of love can also be seen in many famous Christian individuals, for example, the work of Mother Teresa.

Family
Revised ☐

Family life has changed dramatically over the last 40 years. There are now single-parent families and **re-constituted families** as well as **nuclear families**. Nowadays most people have sex before marriage. According to the Office for National Statistics, marriage is at its lowest rate ever; in 2008 it was at its lowest rate since records began. **Cohabitation** has increased in popularity and the average age for marriage has therefore risen. All of these factors mean that instead of the single ideal family (two parents and one child) we now have a variety of possible ways to define a family unit.

> **Re-constituted family** – a family that consists of two parents who have children from previous relationships living together as a family unit.
>
> **Nuclear family** – the traditional ideal of an immediate family, consisting of parents and children.
>
> **Cohabitation** – when two people in a relationship live together without being married.

Scripture-based ideas

The Bible has many examples of the family unit but it is very much culturally influenced in terms of how that unit is understood. For example, the Old Testament seems to allow polygamy and there are clear examples of extended family units under ancient tribal ways of life.

However, it is clear that parents are to be role models for children and are to be respected. This is highlighted in the Ten Commandments: 'Honour your father and your mother' (Exodus 20:12).

In the New Testament the idea of the Christian community as family can be seen in such writings as the Acts of the Apostles (Acts 2:44–47).

Institutional-based ideas: teachings from the Christian Church

Family life is important in Christianity because it is based on the institution of marriage. Procreation is seen to be the next step after marriage, and once a child is born, the Church can be heavily involved in its upbringing.

When family conflicts arise, Christian teachings such as compassion, forgiveness and guidance are applied in order to support people. For example, if ever a marriage was under pressure then it is not unknown for a religious leader to help the couple reconcile. Alternatively, the leader can do the same if there are any problems with the relationships between parents and children. Overall, the family is seen to be a basic building block of society and is seen to assist in stabilising society.

The church community is like an extended family, offering support and offering guidance in times of need. The sacraments of baptism, communion and confirmation demonstrate this as well as godparents – who probably go to the same church and hold some responsibility for the children's religious education.

The church also provides a stable and secure environment for a child with clear ethical guidelines. It offers a sense of belonging to a special community. Children can find like-minded friends through youth clubs, weekend activities and Sunday-school lessons. Often this sense of community carries on through life, sometimes with generations of families belonging to the same church.

Individual-based ideas

As with marriage, the idea of the family within Christianity has taken on board a more modern perspective. Some Christians are part of family units that fall outside the traditional nuclear unit. Single parent and reconstituted families are accepted within the Christian tradition with its focus on forgiveness, reconciliation, tolerance and acceptance. Everyone is seen as an individual before God according to Christian teaching. Every individual has access to the love of God.

Exam tip

For an AO1 answer, be selective with your material. The examination is measuring your skill of demonstrating how much you understand and can explain, not how much you can remember.

Now test yourself

Tested ☐

9 Outline two Scripture-based beliefs about love **or** family.
10 Give two different individual views on family to show how they can differ within Christianity.

Answers on page 107

Typical mistake

Candidates often produce lists of information without examples or developing their explanation/ evaluation.

Issues arising

Because religious teaching is rooted in history, is it ever relevant to people today?

Revised ☐

One of the main objections to the role of religion today is that it is based on a very dated worldview. Many people see it as a product of historical and social contexts. Here are some ideas to consider:

Relevant	Irrelevant
• The importance and popularity of tradition cannot be underestimated. • Religious teaching is one of the main purposes of religious books. • There is a natural law and an order, and because this was established by God, it is equally relevant today as it was when the Bible was written. • The desire of many for religious ceremonies shows that not only is religion still popular but also that its role is seen as significant. • Traditional teachings offered by religion are often seen as a vehicle to create stability for society. • Religious teaching is not set in stone – it has adapted over the years in dealing with issues, for example, divorce, remarriage and homosexuality, without losing a sense of identity or continuity.	• Marriage ceremonies are ancient and custom- or culture-based and they are being adapted into neutral, secular ceremonies. • Religious teaching about children and the purpose of marriage is outdated today on the grounds of an individual's right to choose. • The view of a large part of the Church with regard to the issue of homosexuality is very dated. • Many of the ideas and teachings about sexuality and human relationships are open to interpretation by individual Christians and up for debate between denominations. • As people are living longer, it could be argued that it is impractical to commit to a lifelong relationship. • Some Scriptural teachings are impossible to apply universally today because of the law and human rights, for example, the teaching that practising homosexuals should be put to death. • Some ideas within religion are sexist, for example, the exclusion of women from key roles in the Church.

Exam tip

When answering a question involving AO2, assessment and evaluation, try to draw out both the strengths and weaknesses from a variety of sources.

Typical mistake

If candidates do not have more than two viewpoints to evaluate, their argument is limited.

Whether sexual behaviour is a matter that religion should concern itself with

Revised ☐

The problem with sexuality is that it is a very sensitive and personal issue. Many feel that such issues should not be a matter for institutionalised religion but rather for personal choice and freedom without judgement. Some ideas to consider include the following:

Concern	No concern
• Religion concerns all aspects of life. • Religion celebrates sexuality and does not see it as taboo. • Religion has a lot to say about the positive aspects of sexuality. • Religion has to be involved with ethical concerns because if unchallenged, many problems may occur – religion cannot 'turn a blind eye'.	• Religion is public and sexuality is private – for the religious believer God is the ultimate judge. • Belief is a matter for the individual – it would be inconsistent to say one belief is a matter for the individual but another is not. • Religious teachings are outdated. • Religious teachings can be oppressive and stifling, causing deep-rooted problems such as personality disorders, psychiatric problems and feelings of guilt. • Religious teachings can be seen to be discriminative and offensive.

Typical mistake

Avoid including too much descriptive material without discussion by checking you have evaluated or commented on the significance of the material in each paragraph that you write.

Is modern society setting its own codes of behaviour, and is religion simply trying to adapt to them?

The other side of the argument is that society has already rejected religion and is establishing its own set of rules and codes for behaviour. Some of the points raised here could include:

Points in favour	Points against
• Modern society has moved away from (old) religious teaching. • Modern society is contrary to religious teaching. • Modern society has developed new ideas about relationships and sexuality. • Christian denominations are changing their views.	• Roman Catholic teaching is very much constant. • Modern society has re-interpreted traditional values. • New ideas cannot be adapted to fit traditional values. • Natural law does not change.

Exam tip

Remember that this part of the examination process involves assessment or evaluation, so make sure that you include your own argument in response to the material presented.

Typical mistake

Some candidates simply state a 'for' and 'against' argument without actually commenting on it themselves to demonstrate a process of reasoning that then informs their conclusion.

Now test yourself

11 Outline two arguments as to why the teaching of religion may not be relevant today when it comes to human relationships.

12 Outline two different examples of how it may be argued that religion is adapting to the modern day.

13 State one argument for and one against the view that sexual matters are private and no concern of religion.

Answers on page 107

Exam practice

(a) Explain a religious view about relationships. **(30 marks)**

(b) 'Religion can have no role in the modern world regarding relationships.' Assess this view. **(20 marks)**

Answers online

4 Science and technology

The role of ethics

How far do science and technology need to be controlled through ethical debate? There have been major breakthroughs in science and technology in the last few decades, for example, in medical technology and the field of embryo research. Nonetheless, this has often been the outcome of some form of experimentation, whether human or animal based, and it is this aspect that raises concerns for ethical debate.

Experimentation (animals)

Animals are used mainly in medical and cosmetic research. Medical research covers many areas: behaviour, dissection, the testing of new drugs and the investigation of cures. Cosmetic testing involves testing the safety of chemical-based components in toiletries and beauty products.

There are often conflicting sources and statistics from different organisations about the methods and results of animal experimentation, each with their own agenda. Some examples follow below.

Animal Aid   Revised ☐

Animal Aid was founded in 1977 and 'the society campaigns against all animal abuse but particularly the use of animals in experiments and the cruel treatment of farm animals'. One of the issues it has with animal research is the lack of accuracy in results. Even apes, which can be as little as one per cent genetically different to human beings, can produce significantly different results to them. It also claims that:

- much medical research, including into diseases like cancer, is repetitive and pointless
- we have enough drugs – only 200 are necessary to human health and yet 18,000 versions are tested independently
- the World Health Organisation estimates 80 per cent of cancers are preventable; we should eliminate causes rather than trying to find cures.

Alternatives proposed by Animal Aid

- **In vitro tests**: Scientists can examine human cells or tissues in test tubes in order to study disease, test drugs and manufacture vaccines. Every human cell type can now be studied in vitro.

- Computer models: These can be used to screen potential drugs at an early stage in their development.
- Clinical studies: These involve the monitoring of illnesses in human patients.
- Epidemiology: This is the study and comparison of groups of people to learn what causes health problems.
- Post-mortem studies: Examining the bodies of people who have died can give clues about diseases and their causes.
- Prevention: It makes sense to stop people getting ill in the first place. Educating people about healthy living could save many lives.

In vitro tests – tests done on human cells and tissues in test tubes.

Despite such protests, there have been major breakthroughs in medical history that could not have been achieved without animal experimentation:

Date	Medical breakthrough
1920s	Insulin for diabetics
1930s	Modern anaesthetics
1940s	Whooping cough vaccine
1950s	Kidney transplants; cardiac pacemakers; polio vaccine
1960s	Rubella vaccine; coronary bypass operations; heart transplants; drugs to treat mental illness
1970s	Drugs for ulcers, asthma, leukaemia
1980s	Drugs for viral disease; life-support systems for premature babies

Indeed it is for such reasons that animal research centres, such as Huntingdon Life Sciences Centre, established in 1951, have continued to this day despite being the victims of crimes of terrorism from extreme animal rights campaigners. However, there have been several instances of undercover campaigners' infiltration that have revealed evidence of animal cruelty in experimentation. Such evidence needs to be considered, for example, the use of cats, dogs and primates in what is deemed 'unnecessary' experimentation at the hands of inadequately qualified or incompetent technicians.

Role of ethics in decision-making

Revised

Although they cannot 'talk' this does not mean animals cannot suffer or communicate their suffering. Animals do not and cannot give their consent and it is because of this that they are not given the same rights as a human being. Often the argument of 'the greater good' or 'the lesser of evils' is presented, such as when depriving chimpanzees of their newborns helped outlaw the practice of separation of human babies from their mothers at birth. However, this is not morally convincing.

Peter Singer, philosopher and renowned animal rights campaigner, has long fought for equal rights for animals on the grounds that to deny them such rights is **speciesism**. To disregard animal suffering while concerning oneself with human suffering, is, according to Singer, a form of racism.

> **Speciesism** – the belief that human beings are better than other species.

> **Exam tip**
> Always explain at least two different viewpoints concerning an issue you are studying.

> **Typical mistake**
> Some candidates are tempted to only give their own opinion – do not do this. Try to remain objective.

> **Key quotes**
>
> 'To discriminate against beings solely on account of their species is a form of prejudice.'
>
> (Peter Singer, philosopher)
>
> 'The question is not, can they reason? Nor, can they talk? But can they suffer?'
>
> (Jeremy Bentham, philosopher)
>
> 'If we are willing to conduct experiments on animals we should be willing to do so on humans. These experiments cause pain and we are happy to cause such pain for food, clothes and experimentation in the case of animals. If we are to be consistent and fair we should do the same to humans or not at all.'
>
> (Peter Singer)

> **Now test yourself**
>
> 1 Give one argument Animal Aid gives for stopping animal experimentation.
>
> 2 Name two breakthroughs that have been made by animal experimentation.
>
> 3 What does Peter Singer argue?
>
> **Answers on page 107**
>
> Tested

A religious perspective

According to Genesis, animals were created before human beings and it is part of human beings' responsibility as stewards to look after and care for them. Some Christians become vegetarians because of this responsibility; others (whether vegetarian or not) feel it is important to prevent the loss of animal habitats, unnecessary killing and cosmetic testing on animals.

Unfortunately, throughout history human beings have been cruel towards the animals and Earth God created. Even the Christian Church has not always cared about animal rights in the past. Genesis 1:26 describes human beings as ruling over all creatures that inhabit the Earth. An alternative rendering for 'rule' is '**dominion**', used in some Bible translations. Whichever translation is used, some Christians use this to argue that animals are under our control. That they are not believed to have souls has a major influence on beliefs concerning animal research and vegetarianism. The soul is seen as a divine spark, often the connection between a person and God, and unique and distinct to human beings. Human beings can therefore make decisions about animals and their lives.

> **Dominion** – the idea that human beings are in control of the planet.

While Christians could not possibly advocate torture or cruelty, they could perhaps use these ideas to justify domesticating animals, zoos, the meat industry and the use of animals in medical research. Indeed, it was God who first slaughtered animals: 'The Lord God made garments of skin for Adam and his wife and clothed them' (Genesis 3:21). It was also God who demanded sacrifice throughout the Old Testament, for example, a ram instead of Isaac (Genesis 22:8). Some Christians argue that medical testing which benefits human beings is acceptable as its results are the lesser of two evils.

The Roman Catholic Church believes that animals are below human beings, but its teaching focuses on the duties human beings have towards animals. It therefore would always put human rights above those of animals.

Quakers believe they should show consideration to all of God's creatures. They try to balance the rights of human beings with kindness towards animals, and attempt to bring about the good of both.

> **Exam tip**
>
> If there is not one single opinion within a religion, it is important to point out the variety of viewpoints.

> **Typical mistake**
>
> Candidates sometimes simply present an argument that would not be accepted by all groups within a particular religion.

Now test yourself

4 Why are animals different to human beings according to Roman Catholic teaching?

5 Explain the Christian view on the treatment of animals.

6 Give one argument why animal experimentation may be necessary according to some Christians.

Answers on page 107

Experimentation (human beings)

Human experimentation is less prevalent in modern times, but is certainly not obsolete. It conjures up grisly images of Nazi experimentation and torture, although there are other areas where human participation has been important. Psychology often makes use of behaviour studies, and observation has long been a science implemented in anthropology. Drug testing on human beings has also been a feature of medical and chemical research, but not without its problems, mistakes and concerns.

The major issue here is inconsistency of approach. Some countries and institutions strictly regulate such research; others do not. There is also an ethical concern regarding forced and willing participants, and whether or not those who are paid are fully aware of the risks. It is not uncommon for college and university students to use human subjects for research. But what are the reasons for experimenting on human beings?

- Human experimentation extends human knowledge and enhances human welfare.
- International emergencies, such as war, mean that research is a patriotic imperative to save lives, for example, trying to counter such atrocities as biological weapons.
- The end justifies the means, so individuals can be sacrificed for the good of the majority.

- Human beings must be used to get the most accurate results.
- Freedom of enquiry is essential for optimal results.

Legal human experimentation needs to be controlled by strict regulations and be in line with human rights. Examples include:

- drug trials
- psychological behaviour studies
- medical research through treatments and observation.

As well as flagrant abuses of human rights in illegal human experimentation, there are also cases of mistakes being made in legal human experiments, such as the use of thalidomide to combat morning sickness in pregnancy from the late 1950s until 1961, which caused thousands of children to be born with severe abnormalities. Do the ends really justify the means?

Now test yourself | Tested

7 Give three examples of legal human experimentation.

Answers on page 107

Role of ethics in decision-making | Revised

In the last century there were enormous breakthroughs in medicine, for example, the discovery of penicillin by Alexander Fleming, which saved thousands of lives at the end of the Second World War. However, there have also been mistakes with far-reaching consequences, and this is why science needs the conscience that is ethics to decide upon the best way forward. Advances in science and technology must be maintained within the parameters of human moral behaviour. To allow advancements to exceed these parameters would be irresponsible.

The role of ethics, then, is to ensure ethical practices are followed:

- Scientists and researchers should act ethically and be bound by ethical duty.
- Doctors have a duty to conform to the **Hippocratic Oath**, which begins 'first do no harm'.

- Patient safety must come before financial gain.
- Concealing potentially damaging evidence is immoral.
- The government should have an ethical obligation to regulate experimentation and the use of science and technology in order to protect the public.
- The public must have confidence in the suggested treatments, otherwise they may do themselves more harm by avoiding treatment or applying unsafe treatment.
- Ethics must be in control regarding experiments and new inventions as human beings have a duty to protect and maintain human rights.

Hippocratic Oath – an oath taken by doctors who promise to treat every person and only promote health and well-being through treatments.

Although the field of social science appears more open and collaborative between observer and volunteer, it is recommended that the researcher should consider:

- the ethical nature of the activity
- the potential humiliation or psychological damage that may be caused
- whether the experiment could result in detrimental change to personality or moral character, possibly irreversible in nature
- if any aspect of the experiment or actions involved mislead and support false conclusions.

Although doing the above would potentially eliminate illegality or immoral actions, the integrity of involved parties also needs to be considered, for example, the motives of those giving grants or sponsorships.

Now test yourself   Tested ☐

8   Why is the work of Alexander Fleming important?
9   Explain two ways in which ethics can ensure that ethical practices are followed.

Answers on page 107

> **Exam tip**
>
> This topic is full of new concepts. In your revision, after compiling a glossary of key words, use the terms to draw a flowchart that links each aspect of the topic together. This will help to demonstrate 'good understanding' of the topic overall (AO1).

> **Typical mistake**
>
> Sometimes candidates start to explain one thing but then move away from the focus of the question. Stay focused on the question.

A religious perspective   Revised ☐

Christian beliefs include that God created the natural world to work according to a particular order, although God can intervene through miracles. Nonetheless, Christians accept that God gave us this order to reason and create new technologies and advancements in science in order to further the common good of humanity and work towards eradicating human suffering. The crucial question is, however, how far should the 'hand of science and technology' interfere with the 'hand of the divine'?

Christians accept the Hippocratic Oath and the guidelines for medical ethics drawn up by the General Assembly of the World Medical Association following Nazi abuses. Christians believe the following:

- Human beings are created in the image of God.
- Human beings have a special relationship with God.
- Human beings cannot be used as a 'means to an end' if they are God's unique creation.
- Human beings are to love one another as Jesus loved them.
- Only God can determine the fate of an individual.
- The concept of stewardship involves effort and energy to ensure human life and creation is cared for.

Such teachings clearly limit the parameters of human experimentation.

> **Key quotes**
>
> 'Do to others what you would have them do to you.'
>
> (The Golden Rule, Matthew 7:12)
>
> '"Love the Lord your God with all your heart and with all your soul and with all your strength and with all your mind", and "Love your neighbour as yourself."'
>
> (The Greatest Commandment, Luke 10:27)
>
> 'Then God said, "Let us make man in our image, in our likeness ..." So God created man in his own image.'
>
> (Genesis 1:26–27)

> **Exam tip**
>
> The use of Biblical quotations, where relevant, is a way of clearly illustrating support for a Christian viewpoint.

> **Typical mistake**
>
> Candidates sometimes mistakenly think that the Golden Rule and the Greatest Commandment are found in the Ten Commandments.

Inventions

The development of nuclear power is just one of the countless examples of advancements and inventions over the years – but one which raises serious ethical issues. For example, nuclear fusion has enabled scientists to develop the technology to create weapons of mass destruction. The use of atomic bombs and their aftermath in Nagasaki and Hiroshima illustrate the importance of ethics in controlling the use of such devastating power.

The so-called nuclear arms race has been a significant feature of recent history, with many nations making massive financial commitments to developing this further by way of a 'deterrent' and for 'protection' of their country.

Role of ethics in control of their use
Revised

The rules of conflict such as those found in the **just war** theory are crucial in considering how best to control the development of nuclear weapons. The idea of a just war has been debated for centuries. It would be incorrect to identify the just war theory as a single theory; it has developed from simple ideals to a complex range of proposals. The original questions of when it was right to go to war and how to fight in a war have developed into two main areas of the theory of a just war. In response to modern conflicts much of this has been re-evaluated and developed.

> **Just war** – the theory that war, although potentially an evil, can actually be justified as the lesser of evils if strict rules are followed.

The first aspect is *jus ad bellum*, that is, the reasoning for war, of which there are six requirements:

1 Just cause: war has to be for the right reason. The ideas of right reason and just cause cover self-defence, defending others from attack and protecting the innocent.

2 Right intention: even if a just cause can be established, the motive has to be pure. Power, finance, land or revenge are examples of wrong motives.

3 Proper authority and public declaration: the leader must declare war and do so publicly.

4 Last resort: all other diplomatic negotiations must have failed. Every attempt to resolve the matter peacefully must have been unsuccessful.

5 Probability of success: some see this as biased against smaller countries, but in practice the principle of self-defence over-rides it.

6 Proportionality: it is only sensible to weigh up the probability that greater good is going to come from the war. The benefits need to be worth the devastating costs the war may bring.

It is clear that the use of nuclear weapons do not conform to any of these and in fact contravene a crucial part of the second aspect of *jus in bello*, that is, conduct during conflict: no means that are *mala in se* – no methods or weapons that are 'evil in themselves' – may be used.

Exam practice answers at **www.therevisionbutton.co.uk/myrevisionnotes**

A religious perspective

Some Christians are totally against violence and war based on the principles found in the Ten Commandments like 'you shall not kill' (Exodus 20:13), and Jesus' teaching that 'he who lives by the sword will die by the sword' (Matthew 26:52). Some argue that violence can be justified by referring to Biblical battles; however, nuclear weapons could neither be supported nor justified on this Old Testament basis. Ultimately, Jesus taught a way of peace, love and reconciliation, saying 'blessed are the peacemakers' and the majority of Christians would take this line of reasoning.

In supporting the just war theory, some Christians would reason that the use of nuclear weapons, due to their devastating and far-reaching impact, could never be justified.

Exam tip

Always remember to show that you understand a topic by avoiding lists in your answer; be more selective and explain how the different aspects you have selected are relevant to the answer. This demonstrates that 'information is accurate and relevant' (AO1).

Typical mistake

Make sure that in an exam you use your technical information correctly. Do not confuse key terms.

Now test yourself

Tested

10 Explain the difference between *jus ad bellum* and *jus in bello*.

11 Give two Christian teachings that would be used against war.

Answers on page 107

Scientific and technological advances

There has been much debate recently about the use of embryos in medical research, the use of stem cells provided by embryos that have been generated by such research, the use of technology to provide infertility treatments and the use of cloning.

IVF – in vitro fertilisation describes the human egg being fertilised by the sperm outside of the body.

Embryo research

This involves use of human embryos that are a by-product of **IVF**, donated by couples for medical testing purposes. Legally, they can only be used up to 14 days. Although they were not initially harvested with the aim of use in medical research, they have provided science with the potential to find a cure for degenerative disorders. IVF treatment itself was the outcome of such research.

More recent work has been done with stem cells at a very early stage to try to discover ways of combatting degenerative diseases such as Alzheimer's, Parkinson's and Huntington's. Such work is carried out under strict guidelines, and it must not:

● mix human and animal embryos

● alter the genetic structure of cells in an embryo

● carry out human cloning (replacing the nucleus of a cell with that of another human being).

Cloning

A clone is a genetically identical copy of an animal or human being. There are two types of processes:

● Therapeutic cloning creates genetically identical organs and stem cells for medical purposes such as gene therapy and the treatment of degenerative diseases.

● Reproductive cloning is when a full human being is cloned in order to solve reproductive problems for individuals by replacing the stem cells with the appropriate genetic materials. It is currently illegal in the UK.

Decisions about who benefits

Therapeutic cloning will enable those who suffer from degenerative diseases to eventually benefit through the development of radical new treatments. However, there is a shortage of donated organs to work from and so the UK parliament has been actively working to adapt current regulations to assist scientists in advancing this new work.

The Human Fertilisation and Embryology Authority (HFEA) strictly regulates the work into embryo research and a licence will only be granted for embryo research if 'it is satisfied that the use of human embryos is necessary or desirable for the purposes of the research and may only be allowed for one of the following purposes:

● to promote advances in the treatment of infertility

● to increase knowledge about the causes of congenital disease

● to increase knowledge about the cause of miscarriages

● to develop more effective techniques of contraception

● to develop methods for detecting the presence of gene or chromosome abnormalities.'

A religious perspective

There is no specific teaching in the Bible about treating infertility. Three quotations from the Old Testament give an indication that it is God's will and possibly some form of punishment:

● But Abram said, 'O Sovereign Lord, what can you give me since I remain childless . . . ?' (Genesis 15:2)

● Rachael cried to her husband, Jacob: 'Give me children, or I'll die!'. (Genesis 30:1)

● 'Peninnah had children, but Hannah had none . . . and the Lord had closed her womb.' (1 Samuel 1:2–5)

There is certainly disparity from the Christian perspective when it comes to views about fertility treatments and the experiments upon which they are based. Today, the Roman Catholic Church teaches that artificial insemination violates the dignity of the person and threatens the sanctity of marriage. It argues that IVF treatment opposes both natural and divine law. Indeed, a third party being involved in the marriage is like adultery. It could also be a problem because in **AID** (Artificial Insemination by Donor) treatment, the genetic father has no responsibility for the child. Just as with the above quotes from the Old Testament the Roman Catholic Church teaches that the matter of fertility is down to the will of God.

> **AID** – Artificial Insemination by Donor.
>
> **AIH** – Artificial Insemination by Husband.

Protestant traditions are more open to debate. As infertility treatment is in harmony with the purpose of marriage – to have a family – it is generally acceptable, although some prefer **AIH** (Artificial Insemination by Husband) to AID.

> **Exam tip**
>
> Make sure that you are specific about which denomination within a religion teaches what. It is important to be precise.

Now test yourself

12 What is the HFEA and what does it do?

13 Why is AID not an acceptable practice for the Roman Catholic Church?

Answers on page 107

> **Typical mistake**
>
> Some candidates write as if there is only one view from within a religion and this is never the case.

Exam practice answers at **www.therevisionbutton.co.uk/myrevisionnotes**

Human rights

The Universal Declaration of Human Rights (UDHR) was established in 1948. It states 30 human rights of which several are pertinent to the use of modern technology: basic equality, the right to have human rights, freedom from slavery and torture, equality under the law, and freedoms to express oneself in terms of conscience, opinion and thought.

The conflict with the use of technology — Revised

With the advancement in the use of technology, three areas have often been debated:

● use of the internet or **cyber crime**

● data protection

● privacy.

With the use of the world wide web and advancements in computer technology it is easy to see how the human rights advocated by UDHR, and especially Article 12, can be abused. Personal data stored by banks and companies can be leaked, and identities stolen.

As well as these obvious cyber crimes, there are also fundamental issues concerning the basic protection of personal, sensitive data and the right of an individual to privacy, for example, mass surveillance through data collection and storage or through CCTV cameras.

Liberty (founded 1934) is a movement that aims to protect an individual's freedoms and rights in line with the UDHR. For example, it has questioned the use of data by corporations and challenged the idea of a national database and identity card scheme.

> **Key quotes**
>
> 'Everyone is entitled to all the rights and freedoms set forth in this Declaration, without distinction of any kind, such as race, colour, sex, language, religion, political or other opinion, national or social origin, property, birth, or other status. Furthermore, no distinction shall be made on the basis of the political, jurisdictional or international status of the country or territory to which a person belongs whether it be independent, trust, non-self-governing or under any other limitation of sovereignty.'
>
> (Article 2, UDHR)
>
> 'No one shall be subjected to arbitrary interference with this privacy, family, home or correspondence, nor to attacks upon his honour and reputation. Everyone has the right to the protection of the law against such interference or attacks.'
>
> (Article 12, UDHR)

> **Cyber crime** – crime involving use of a computer and a network, including the internet.

A religious perspective — Revised

The issue of human rights is close to the heart of the Christian Gospel. Jesus taught that everyone is equal and that no one should be discriminated against. The Bible teaches that God cares for everyone and instructs societies to be responsible and non-oppressive. Such teachings are used by Christians to argue that personal freedom is God-given, and to challenge that would be to challenge God.

> **Exam tip**
>
> You must be selective when answering a question. Remember, select the 'relevant and appropriate' information. You cannot include everything.

> **Typical mistake**
>
> Candidates sometimes do not include examples to help explain the points they make (AO1) or back up their arguments with evidence (AO2).

> **Now test yourself** — Tested
>
> 14 What is the UDHR?
> 15 What is Liberty and what does it do?
>
> Answers on page 107

Issues arising

Should science be controlled by ethics, and if so, which ethical system?

Revised

Each ethical system could potentially give a very different outcome. If there is disagreement about the ethical approach, how can this work?

Control	No control
<ul><li>History teaches us that science and technology do need controlling, for example, the terrible experimentation by the Nazis.</li><li>We need to protect society from any further abuse.</li><li>No control would mean 'anything goes' and create chaos, immoral activity and the use of science and technology could get out of control.</li><li>We must think about the future of our planet.</li><li>Ethical theories provide clear guidance and most agree on technology issues so it would be an effective way of avoiding all the potential problems.</li></ul>	<ul><li>Control just creates a strict Big Brother society.</li><li>Ethical theories conflict with each other, so how can there be control? Natural law is very strict whereas **situation ethics** is more open and adaptable to new ideas.</li><li>People fear the unknown and the new. If we are too cautious, science and technology cannot advance.</li></ul>

> **Situation ethics** – American moral theologian Joseph Fletcher's theory that considers each situation before applying the Christian principle of love as guidance for action.

Is it better for ethics to be reactive – to respond to new scientific ideas?

Revised

Again, this question considers whether or not the role of ethics should be integral to the process of scientific investigation. Some would see this as a 'quality control' procedure and thus potentially a way to avoid many ethical dilemmas.

Reactive	Unresponsive
<ul><li>It is in the nature of ethics to be reactive to new ideas.</li><li>Ethics should not be separated from science and technology but be integral to the process.</li><li>Procedures for ethical practice need to be inherent in the fabric of the scientific and technological process and professionals should be obliged to conform.</li><li>Ethics protects and champions human rights.</li></ul>	<ul><li>Ethics has no right to question science.</li><li>Ethics is always catching up and is too far behind new technologies to react effectively.</li><li>Ethics is sometimes an excuse for religious teachings to be aired that are unrepresentative of the majority and so should be kept separate.</li></ul>

> **Exam tip**
> Always refer back to the question in your answers, demonstrating that you are providing 'a well-focused, reasoned response' (AO2).

> **Typical mistake**
> Some candidates simply list arguments without explaining them.

Can a scientific discovery be 'undiscovered'?

Revised

Once something is discovered there is sometimes potential for its exploitation and use in a negative way. This question considers whether or not we can ever prevent this.

No	Yes
● Can the potential use and development of nuclear power be taken away now that it has been discovered? ● Can we eradicate knowledge and move backwards? It is highly unlikely because somebody, somewhere will use it. ● To try to 'undiscover' things is dangerous because it leaves the possibility that someone will abuse it and so it is best to embrace new knowledge and control it ethically.	● The world has been made a worse place through the misuse of advancements. ● The cost of maintaining new discoveries that are so open to abuse is not worth the expense of so much human misery, for example, wars, biological weapons, etc.

Typical mistake

Candidates sometimes write a conclusion that does not link, through a process of reasoning, to the rest of their answer.

How far should society allow religion to control scientific and technological development?

Revised

Religion has a vital role in ethics and some see the involvement of religion with ethics as a positive thing. Others would disagree and argue that religion is always too negative.

Religion to provide control	Religion to be uninvolved
● There has been a great history of religious involvement in ethical issues. ● It is vital because ethical issues are fundamental to religion. ● God directs religious views and so it has to be right for religion to be involved. ● Much religious involvement is from an ethical perspective. ● Secular control can be driven by materialism.	● Religion is separate from science. ● Religious involvement only encourages negative criticism. ● Religious involvement attracts fundamentalist views that are often contrary to public opinion. ● Most states are secular today. ● Religion is outdated. ● Which religion? Which interpretation? This debate could hinder progress.

Now test yourself

Tested

16 Why should ethics be used to control science and technology?

17 Give one reason why a scientific discovery cannot be 'undiscovered'.

18 Explain one argument for the involvement of religion in the control of science and technology.

Answers on page 107

Exam tip

Try to build up your argument for evaluation answers by giving more than one reason for a viewpoint along with some sort of explanation or justification.

Exam practice

(a) Explain arguments for and against the use of human beings **or** animals in experiments. (30 marks)

(b) 'Without experiments science would never advance and the human race would suffer.' Assess this claim. (20 marks)

Answers online

Online

Typical mistake

Candidates sometimes do not consider views other than their own.

1 The ontological argument: faith and reason

The ontological argument

Arguments to prove God's existence have rested on two main approaches. The first starts from the experience of the world, and draws inferences from such observations. The cosmological and design arguments take this approach. The second approach, and that of the ontological argument, examines the very concept of God.

Ontological literally means 'concerned with being'. The argument is **deductive** rather than **inductive** in its form. Its premises are a priori, which means that its truth-value is judged without reference to experience or investigation. The argument does not appeal to some feature of the universe but focuses on the concept of God.

> **Deductive** – a process of reasoning by which the conclusion is shown to follow necessarily from the premises.
>
> **Inductive** – a process of reasoning that draws a general conclusion from specific instances.

Exam tip

This topic is full of new concepts. In your revision, after compiling a glossary of key words, use the terms to draw a flowchart that links each aspect of the topic together.

Anselm
Revised

Anselm (1033–1109) was a philosopher and theologian who became Archbishop of Canterbury. His argument attempted to show that the concept of God included the concept of existence. His argument was in two forms.

The first form: God has existence in reality

Anselm began by defining God as 'a being than which nothing greater can be conceived'. It is possible to think of something greater than a mere idea. If God is the greatest, then he must really exist separately from people's imaginations. He must exist in reality. Therefore, the concept of God must include actual existence.

As an argument:

● God is the greatest possible being (nothing greater can be conceived).

● If God exists in the mind alone (only as an idea) then a greater being could be imagined to exist, both in the mind and in reality.

● This being would then be greater than God.

● Thus God cannot exist only as an idea in the mind.

● Therefore, God must exist both in the mind, as an idea, and in reality.

Anselm is *not* saying 'because I think of God he must exist'. Rather, 'it is when I think about him I realise the necessity of God's existence. Existence imposes itself on my thoughts – rather than my thoughts imposing existence on God'.

Typical mistake

Candidates often begin their account of Anselm's ontological argument with a lengthy paragraph recounting irrelevant biographical details. Marks are awarded for the demonstration of an understanding of the arguments, not for potted biographies.

Now test yourself

1 What is Anselm's definition of God?

2 What aspect of the first form of Anselm's ontological argument makes it a deductive argument?

Answers on page 107

Tested

Exam practice answers at **www.therevisionbutton.co.uk/myrevisionnotes**

The second form: God has necessary existence

Gaunilo of Marmoutiers was an eleventh-century Benedictine monk who challenged the first form of Anselm's argument by basically saying 'if you conceive of the greatest of anything then it seems that it must have to exist, on the grounds that it is greater to exist in reality than in the mind only'. Gaunilo used the example of 'the greatest conceivable lost island' and contended that by Anselm's reasoning the lost island must exist, and so Anselm's argument must be flawed.

Anselm's reply became the second form of the argument. He argued that God is a different order of being. There are two types of existence: existence that can fail to be (contingent existence) and existence that cannot fail to be (necessary existence). God cannot come and go out of existence. It was impossible to conceive of God as not existing. God not only exists but also has necessary existence.

Hence, the ontological argument is only applicable to God.

As an argument:

- God is the greatest possible being so nothing greater can be conceived.
- It is greater to be a **necessary being** than a **contingent being**.
- If God exists only as a contingent being, so therefore can be imagined not to exist, then a greater being can be imagined, namely a necessary being.
- This necessary being would be greater than God.
- Therefore God must be a necessary being, and exist in reality.

> **Necessary being** – a being that, if it exists, cannot not exist, whose non-existence would be self-contradiction.
>
> **Contingent being** – a being that need not be, that could have been different; something that has dependency.

Now test yourself — Tested

3 What is the difference between a contingent being and a necessary being?

4 Why is Gaunilo's challenge said to fail?

Answers on page 107

Typical mistake

Candidates often only give part of Anselm's arguments. Remember that Anselm's ontological argument comes in two forms.

Descartes — Revised

The philosopher René Descartes (1596–1650) distinguished between a thing's essence and its existence. He argued it was possible to determine what something was (its essence) independently of knowing whether it existed. Descartes defined God as a supremely perfect being with **omniscience** and **omnipotence**. However, all of these properties would be meaningless without existence. Thus, for Descartes, existence is inseparable from the essence of God. He likened this to the idea of a triangle that could not be separated from the idea of three angles adding up to 180 degrees. The idea of a perfect being demanded the **predicate** of existence, since existence is an aspect of perfection. In all cases apart from God, essence is different from existence. Like Anselm's argument, the very concept of God imposes necessary existence.

> **Omniscience** – the ability to know everything; all-knowing.
>
> **Omnipotence** – the power to do anything; all-powerful. Some philosophers exclude the logically impossible.
>
> **Predicate** – something that adds to our concept of the subject.

As an argument:

- God, a supremely perfect being, has all perfections.
- Existence is a perfection.
- Therefore God, a supremely perfect being, must exist.

Differences between Anselm and Descartes

Anselm and Descartes may appear to make similar points; however, their arguments are very different.

Anselm	Descartes
There is no theory of absolute greatness. It is more that existing in reality is greater than existing as an idea.	There is the idea of absolute objective perfection.
Existence in reality is greater when compared to existence that is in the mind only. There is no concept of total greatness of which existence is an aspect.	Existence is an aspect of the concept of total perfection.
Existence is not a predicate. It does not add to our concept of the subject.	Existence is a predicate. It adds to our concept of the subject. It is an attribute.

More recent forms

Revised

There are numerous modern forms of the ontological argument. The most popular ones focus on necessary existence and **possible worlds**.

Norman Malcolm: necessary existence

Necessary existence is defined as existence that cannot be brought about or threatened by anything. Thus, God's existence is either impossible or necessary. It cannot be impossible since the concept is not self-contradictory. Therefore, God necessarily exists.

Alvin Plantinga: possible worlds

The idea of possible worlds is a method used by philosophers to determine the modality (necessity, impossibility or possibility) of statements. Hence, this formulation of the ontological argument has become known as the **modal** form. To test for logical impossibility, you need to think of a possible world in which the statement is true. If you can, then the statement is not logically impossible. For a statement to be logically necessary it would be true in all possible worlds. So the ontological argument is as follows:

- There are possible worlds, and in one of these there exists a being with maximal greatness and excellence (having the properties of omniscience, omnipotence, etc.).
- In any possible world this being has maximal excellence (omniscience, omnipotence, etc.).
- Our world is a possible world (since our world exists).
- Therefore, in our world there is this being.

Possible worlds – a conception of a logically consistent universe that might have been.

Modal – the mode in which something occurs, for example, either necessary or possible.

Now test yourself

Tested

5   Explain two differences between Anselm's and Descartes' ontological arguments.
6   Which of the following are possible worlds? Give reasons to support your answer.
   (a) A world where Colin and Simon are taller than each other at the same time.
   (b) A world where Wayne Rooney is King of Scotland.
   (c) A world where David Cameron is the Prime Minister of the United Kingdom.

Answers on page 107

Objections and responses

1 Definition of God

Revised

Aquinas (1225–1274) argued that we cannot prove that God exists just from the concept or idea of God. We have no way of knowing if our definition of God is correct since God is beyond human understanding.

'The greatest' and 'the most perfect being' are not meaningful concepts. They do not have a maximum. With numbers, you can never come to the end as you can always add one to the last number. In the same way, greatness and perfection can always be added to.

Response

- The definition conveys meaning. Whatever one believes about God, it seems reasonable to say that nothing can be thought to be greater than God.
- Anselm was presenting his definition as a prayer to aid faith rather than as a proof of God.
- Recent forms of the argument using the idea of necessary existence and possible worlds claim that an argument based on a definition is valid. (See section on page 56.)

2 Existence as a predicate of God

Revised

The German philosopher Immanuel Kant (1724–1804) argued that existence is not a real predicate. It does not add to our concept of the subject. To say a concept existed is to state that it had an actuality. For example, to say that a kangaroo exists does not add anything to our concept of a kangaroo. The concept is not made greater or more perfect by asserting that it corresponds to a reality. Existence is not something that can be added to or subtracted from something.

In the sentence 'God exists', the subject is really 'the concept of God', and the predicate is 'applies to something'. When expressed in this way, it can be seen that existence is not a property.

We do not add anything to the concept when we declare that it 'is'. Otherwise it would not be exactly the same thing that exists but something more than we had thought in the concept; and we could not, therefore, say that the exact object of my concept exists.

Response

- Necessary existence is a property of an inability to be generated or made corrupt.
- Philosopher Stephen Davis argued that the mere concept of money does not have the property of enabling him to purchase anything in the real world. Therefore, existence does add a **great-making quality** and permits the purchase of real items in the real world.

Great-making quality – a property that makes an object greater.

3 Deriving existential claims from definition

The argument implies you can define anything into existence – which is absurd. 'Filling out a concept' and 'showing that there really is something to which the concept refers' are two quite different processes and the first does not lead to the second.

Definitions only tell us what God would be like *if* he existed. They cannot establish whether he does in fact exist. One can move from a concept of imagination to a concept of reality, but not from a concept of imagination to reality. For example, describing a unicorn does not make the unicorn exist. See Gaunilo's criticism (page 53).

Response

- Anselm's response was that islands are contingent and therefore do not have necessary existence as an aspect of their properties. However, God does, and is unique in this aspect. Existence is not part of the greatness of an island, whereas necessary existence is part of the concept of God.

- Explaining a concept can make non-existence apparent. For example, 'round squares' cannot exist. Therefore, the two processes of concept and actuality are related, implying that by filling out a concept you can move to actuality.

> **Key quote**
>
> 'A hundred real thalers* do not contain the least coin more than a hundred possible thalers.'
>
> (Immanuel Kant)
>
> *Thaler: an old German silver coin

> **Exam tip**
>
> Challenging a criticism may involve not just explaining why the criticism is weak or fails, but also why the alternative is more persuasive.

> **Now test yourself**
>
>
> 7 Explain Aquinas' argument as to why you cannot prove God exists from the definition of God.
>
> 8 How does Stephen Davis reply to the argument that existence is not a real predicate?
>
> 9 The ontological argument implies you can define anything into existence. Give two arguments that respond to this challenge.
>
> **Answers on page 107**

> **Exam tip**
>
> Make sure that you focus on the question when planning and writing your answer and avoid including irrelevant material.

The relationship between faith and reason

Does understanding follow faith, or is understanding required for faith? Do we need to have some independent reason to believe in something, or does reason hamper true faith?

Since **the Enlightenment**, in order for any religious belief to be viewed as rational it had to be supported by reason. However, some theologians and philosophers, such as Terence Penelhum (b. 1929), draw a distinction between 'wordly wisdom' and 'special revelation': 'to seek to establish God's presence by reason is to attempt to bypass the spiritual regeneration which is the condition of recognising it, and which requires response to his special revelation'.

> **The Enlightenment** – an eighteenth-century philosophical movement that stressed the importance of reason.

Other philosophers such as Søren Kierkegaard (1813–1855) argued that to attempt to use reason to determine whether or not God exists is both misconceived and ridiculous. Kierkegaard said, 'For the fool says in his heart that there is no God, but he who says in his heart or to others: just wait a little and I shall demonstrate it … What a superb theme for crazy comedy'. Kierkegaard thought that using reason on issues such as the existence of God was to go beyond reason's limits.

The various forms of the ontological argument seem to be insufficient to convert the atheist. However, perhaps that was not the original intention. It is likely that Anselm was writing for those who already had a belief in God, and wanted to show that their faith was rational.

In contrast, Descartes was attempting to give a logical argument to prove the existence of God. He required proof of God to justify his rationalistic approach to knowledge and certainty. Recent forms of the ontological argument have also focused on trying to justify belief in God through argument and reason. The existence of God is seen as a proposition that can be supported by argument. Faith is shown to be rational.

Key quote

'I have written the following treatise in the person of one who … seeks to understand what he believes … I do not seek to understand in order to believe but I believe in order to understand. For I believe even this: that I shall not understand unless I believe.'

(Aquinas in the preface to *Proslogion*, 1078, where his ontological argument appears)

The value of the argument for faith

Revised

The value of the argument for faith will depend on how successful the argument is deemed to be, and one's views about the relationship between faith and reason. If viewed as helping understanding from a faith position, then the ontological argument may help the believer in understanding that God has necessary existence. Alternatively, it could be seen as proof that God exists. In that case, the ontological argument could lead someone to a faith in God. Some may claim that certainty is a denial of faith and so the ontological argument could also be viewed negatively.

Key quote

'If I am capable of grasping God objectively, I do not believe, but precisely because I cannot do this I must believe. If I wish to preserve myself in faith I must constantly be intent upon holding fast the objective uncertainty.'

(Kierkegaard)

Now test yourself

Tested

10 Explain the difference between 'understanding in order to believe' and 'believing in order to understand'.

Answers on page 107

Issues arising

Does the ontological argument have any value for the non-believer?

Revised

The section on the relationship between faith and reason (see pages 56–57) will be useful for discussion of this issue.

The key issues to consider are:

(a) Can belief in God be arrived at through reasoned arguments?

If Kierkegaard and Penelhum are correct then the ontological argument will have little value. Coming to a belief in God by means of rational argument alone is beyond the limits of both philosophy and reason. Likewise, if faith is required prior to reason, then the ontological argument will be of little value to the non-believer.

However, if the view of the Enlightenment is correct, then the ontological argument may be of value. It is a deductive argument – if the premises are true, the conclusion must follow and therefore it holds out the hope of a universal proof. It is also an a priori argument since it has no premises acquired from experience so it cannot be refuted **empirically**.

(b) Is the ontological argument successful?

Even if belief in God can be arrived at through reason, the ontological argument only matters to the non-believer if the argument is persuasive. This will then be a case of weighing up the relative strengths and weaknesses. One strength is that it poses a direct challenge to a non-believer, since its starting point is the definition of God. Non-believers must have a concept of God and so may be drawn to the conclusion that God must exist.

> **Exam tip**
>
> Always make sure that you draw a conclusion from the arguments that you have put forward. Your conclusion may be that you cannot reach a clear conclusion because the arguments are finely balanced.

> **Empirical** – anything that is to do with the human senses.

> **Typical mistake**
>
> Candidates often misjudge the time and spend too long on the AO1 question. Remember that the AO2 question is worth 20 marks, and it is important that you allocate the right proportion of time to answer it.

Does it successfully challenge disbelief in God?

Revised

The level of success of the argument's challenge to disbelief in God will depend on how persuasive the ontological argument is perceived to be. The ontological argument points to a God who has necessary existence, but it does not reveal any other aspects of God and so may not describe the God of **classical theism**.

Again, there are issues about faith and reason. For example, can a philosophical argument ever lead to belief in God? To what extent can a philosophical argument lead to **agnosticism** and thus challenge disbelief in God?

> **Classical theism** – the belief in a personal deity, creator of everything that exists, who is distinct from that creation and is sustainer and preserver of the universe.
>
> **Agnosticism** – the belief that it is not possible to know whether God exists.

How successful is the argument as proof of God's existence?

Revised

This issue requires a judgement of the success, or failure, of the arguments and responses listed on pages 55–56. Ask yourself some key questions, for example:

● Does the definition of God make sense? Can you have a concept of the greatest or most perfect being?
● If the ontological argument was meant to be an aid to faith rather than leading to faith, to what extent does it reveal anything about God?
● How successful are the recent formulations of the argument involving possible worlds?
● Is Stephen Davis' example about purchasing power in the real world convincing?
● Was Gaunilo's criticism correct, or are concept and actuality related?

> **Typical mistake**
>
> Candidates often give one-sided evaluations. Always make sure that you consider different views in your evaluation.

Would the success or failure of this argument have any significance for faith?

Revised

You need to analyse the concept of 'religious faith' and consider the consequences for the success or failure of the ontological argument. Some of the material in the first 'issue arising' discussed on page 58 would be relevant here.

Possible areas to consider:

Consequences for faith (success)	Consequences for faith (failure)
Gives reason to believe – leads to or strengthens faith.	May weaken faith as reason for belief fails.
Gives understanding to faith.	Gives no extra understanding to faith, so is not relevant.
Would provide a challenge to the atheist.	May weaken faith as no arguments for God with which to oppose atheists.
Proof would negate faith.	Proof is neither relevant to faith, nor sought after.
The God of philosophy is not the God of classical theism, therefore the argument is irrelevant.	The God of philosophy is not the God of classical theism, therefore the argument is irrelevant.

> **Now test yourself**
>
> Tested
>
> 11 Explain why, if the view of the Enlightenment is correct, the ontological argument may be of value to the non-believer.
>
> 12 Is Gaunilo correct in his criticism of the ontological argument? Give reasons to support your answer.
>
> Answers on page 107

> **Exam practice**
>
> **(a)** Outline Anselm's ontological argument. **(30 marks)**
>
> **(b)** 'The success or failure of the ontological argument has no significance for religious faith.' To what extent do you agree? **(20 marks)**
>
> **Answers online**
>
> Online

2 Religious language

The problem of religious language

'I am writing this chapter of the book in Malta.' By saying this, I am making a statement about the writing of this chapter and claiming it is the case. I am using language that describes part of everyday experience in the real world.

Religious language also seems to make claims that are facts, such as 'God answers prayer', 'Jesus ascended into heaven' or 'God is timeless'. Such claims have moved away from a common shared base and experience, and entered a different realm of language. They use language that is describing things that are over and beyond our world. The language is often related to the **metaphysical** and the mysterious, yet the claims seem to be making statements about the real world.

This creates a problem in that people are no longer sure what is being communicated. For example, the claim that 'God is timeless' is difficult to understand since we only have experiences within the world of time.

> **Metaphysical** – to do with a non-physical realm.

> **Exam tip**
>
> To help you remember all the different approaches to religious language, use flashcards with examples to illustrate each approach.

Meaningfulness   Revised ☐

In the 1920s and 1930s a group of philosophers were concerned that some questions remained unanswered century after century while other academic areas progressed. They wondered whether some philosophical questions were never resolved because they were not real, meaningful questions. This group of philosophers was based in Vienna and became known as the 'Vienna Circle'. Its members mostly had a background in science. The group decided it needed a test for meaningfulness, so that propositions could be identified as either meaningful or meaningless. Note that they were only interested in whether a statement made sense, not whether it was true or false.

There were three major influences that helped shape the Vienna Circle:

Empiricism

The eighteenth-century Scottish philosopher David Hume (1711–1776) argued that any idea we have, however complex, can be reduced to some experience that our senses have provided. Knowledge is based on experience. Apparent knowledge, which is not gained from experience (such as logic and mathematics), is not real knowledge since it tells us nothing about the world itself.

Science

Science provided answers. It resulted in agreed knowledge. The scientific methodology of testing things, of trying to verify by experiment, suggested the key to testing for meaningfulness was verification, that is, showing something is true.

The picture theory

In 1921, the philosopher Ludwig Wittgenstein (1889–1951) published a book called *Tractatus Logico-Philosophicus* in which he presented the picture theory of language. The meaning of a proposition lay in knowing what is pictured. Words ultimately derive from our sensory experience. Meaningful language involved words being defined by the real world of objects.

> **Now test yourself**   Tested ☐
>
> 1 Why does religious language create a problem?
> 2 State three influences that helped shape the thinking of the Vienna Circle.
>
> **Answers on page 108**

> **Typical mistake**
>
> Don't write a long introduction that merely repeats the question or lists the things that you are going to discuss. Your first paragraph needs to pick up the focus of the question immediately.

The verification principle

Revised

The strong form

Logical positivism was a movement that developed from the Vienna Circle. Its proponents sought to find the ultimate test for meaningful statements – the verification principle. For a statement to be meaningful it had to be able to be verified by the sense experiences, in practice and conclusively.

'Meaningful' is concerned with whether a statement makes sense whereas 'meaning' explains what the statement is claiming. The logical positivists saw the two as related and argued that 'the meaning of the statement is the method of verification'. In other words, we know the meaning of a statement if we know the conditions under which the statement is true or false.

> **Logical positivism** – a school of philosophy that emerged out of the Vienna Circle in the early twentieth century.

The weak form

Clearly, the verification principle eliminated historical statements and general laws of science since it was not possible to observe and therefore verify past events or statements that apply universally (for example, water freezes at 0°C). However, such statements were seen as meaningful, so the British philosopher A J Ayer (1910–1989) suggested a weaker form of the logical positivists' argument. He said that religious statements should be:

- verifiable in principle rather than in practice (that is, if you knew how to show it could be true)
- verifiable in terms of 'probable' rather than conclusive (that is, if you knew how to show it was probably true).

However, a religious statement such as 'God is timeless', even by the weak verification principle, was deemed meaningless. Indeed, all talk of God must be nonsensical since 'the notion of a person whose essential attributes are non-empirical is not an intelligible notion at all' (A J Ayer).

The logical positivists argued that through the misuse of language, people assumed that because a word existed there must be some corresponding reality, for example, the word 'God'.

Now test yourself

3   What is the difference between 'meaningful' and 'meaning'?

4   What is the difference between the strong form of the verification principle and the weak form?

Answers on page 108

Tested

The falsification principle

Revised

Sir Karl Popper (1902–1994) challenged this accepted methodology of science and argued that it was concerned with falsification rather than verification: theories are considered true until some evidence counts against them.

The parable of the gardener

The British philosopher Antony Flew (1923–2010) applied this to the debate about language and used a parable (previously used by John Wisdom). He told of two explorers who discover a clearing that resembles a humanly made garden yet in other ways resembles a natural phenomenon. One explorer is convinced that there is a gardener; the other disagrees. They set about testing the hypothesis that there is a gardener, using fences, bloodhounds and so on. No evidence of a gardener turns up. However, at every stage the believer qualifies the hypothesis: the gardener comes at night; he is invisible; he cannot be detected by any of the senses. Finally, the non-believer asks: 'Just how does what you call an invisible, intangible, eternally elusive gardener differ from an imaginary gardener or even no gardener at all?'

Flew's claim is that this is what happens to religious claims.

Religion does not let itself be proven false – there is an answer for every question, in statements like 'God moves in mysterious ways'. For the non-believer there seems to be no difference between a God who loves, a God who does not love and no God at all.

Both Ayer and later John Hick (1922–2012) seem to link this approach of falsification to the test for meaningfulness. If it was known how a statement could be shown to be false, then the statement was meaningful. If nothing could show it to be false, then the statement was meaningless. The parable seems to imply that religious statements are meaningless since the believer does not allow anything to count against the existence of the gardener (God).

However, there is some debate as to whether that is what Flew intended by the parable. Certainly Popper regarded the falsification principle as a test that a statement was scientific rather than whether it was meaningful. Some argue that Flew was questioning the status of religious statements. It is not clear that he regarded religious statements as meaningless, but was more asking about their meaning.

Now test yourself   Tested

5   State the falsification principle.
6   Explain why the falsification principle might challenge the meaningfulness of religious language.

Answers on page 108

Responses to the verification principle

The *University* debate   Revised

Flew's view brought forth a number of responses that were published in the journal *University* (1950–1951) and are referred to as the '*University* debate'.

'Bliks'

The moral philosopher Richard Hare (1919–2002) held that although religious statements are not open to truth or falsity (**non-cognitive**) in the way that literal statements are true or false (**cognitive**), they are important to the result they have on our conduct. He regarded religious statements as 'bliks', which was his term for unfalsifiable convictions. He illustrated this with a parable about an Oxford don who was convinced that all the other dons were trying to poison him. Whatever their behaviour it was seen to be consistent with their aim to kill him. Nothing they did could ever count against his conviction.

Non-cognitive statements – statements that do not communicate knowledge, information or facts and so do not have a truth-value (are not open to being true or false), for example, 'don't steal'.

Cognitive statements – statements that have a truth-value (are either true or false) and so are literal and communicate facts or information, for example, 'Valletta is the capital of Malta'.

Exam practice answers at **www.therevisionbutton.co.uk/myrevisionnotes**

The parable of the freedom fighter

Basil Mitchell (1917–2011) disagreed with Flew and argued that religious statements are not neutral hypotheses. The religious believer displays an attitude of trust. Mitchell illustrated his view with the parable of the freedom fighter. The freedom fighter meets a stranger whom he believes is the secret leader of the resistance movement. Sometimes the stranger appears to be working against the movement, but he is told it is all part of the stranger's plan. The freedom fighter continues to believe the stranger.

Likewise, religious belief continues, often when there seems to be contrary evidence. The believer weighs the evidence and assesses what is the most reasonable and consistent overall view. Faith is a risky business and it is difficult to say how much contrary evidence it requires before it is abandoned.

> **Key quote**
>
> 'A faith which evades critical questions is a faith that lacks confidence, which is not truly assured it has found truth.'
>
> (C S Evans, philosopher)

Eschatological verification   Revised ☐

Some time after the *University* debate, the philosopher John Hick suggested another way in which verifiability can apply to religious statements in his parable about two travellers walking down the same road. One believed that the road led to the celestial city. The other believed that the road went nowhere. Both interpreted signs along the route in different ways. Hick was clearly thinking of theological statements about the existence of heaven and life after death. He was showing that there are limitations to the falsification principle. The celestial city could be verified by the weak verification principle but obviously could not be falsified.

> **Eschatological verification** – the view that some religious statements are verifiable after death (or at the end of time).

Now test yourself   Tested ☐

7 Explain why Hare considered 'bliks' important.

8 How does 'eschatological verification' claim to address the challenge of the verification principle?

Answers on page 108

Different views of religious language

It is now generally agreed that the ideas of 'verification' and 'falsification' are too narrow and do not provide a criterion for establishing meaning. Many philosophers and theologians argue that religious language is more than just a process by which we label things. Language has many different uses and functions. Religious language can function (for example, through analogies) in terms of giving insight and expressing commitment.

Analogical   Revised ☐

An analogy is a comparison between two things with similar or shared characteristics. For example, the word 'good' can be used to describe a meal or a story, even though a good meal is different to a good story. We only have our everyday language to talk about God but certain words, when applied to God, have a different meaning from their everyday use.

Thomas Aquinas

This understanding of analogical religious language was recognised by the philosopher Thomas Aquinas. He argued it was valid because there was a relationship between the world and God, since God created the world and sustains it.

He identified two types of analogy in religious language:

- Analogy of proportion – we understand human power and this helps us understand God's power. He possesses it in proportion to his reality, just as we possess it in proportion to our reality. We don't fully understand God's power but we get an insight.
- Analogy of attribution – based on the idea that many human characteristics are derived from God's characteristics. Therefore, although we don't fully understand God's wisdom, we can gain insight in that human wisdom is a reflection of God's wisdom.

Ian Ramsey

The idea of analogy was discussed again in the twentieth century by the theologian Ian Ramsey (1915–1972).

Ramsey argued that we all have some understanding of the word 'good'. However, if we want to understand God's goodness we need to adapt our model – we need to qualify it and describe God as infinitely good. The effect of this qualifier will lead us on to thinking about God's goodness in greater and greater depth. Eventually, the 'penny will drop' and we will gain an insight into 'infinite goodness'. We cannot express this insight (which Ramsey calls a disclosure) but it is evoked by the qualifier. Ramsey also believed when we gain this insight we will respond to it – it will create a sense of wonder and a sense of commitment.

> **Typical mistake**
>
> A quotation without a comment will not suffice as an explanation. You need to clarify its relevance and say how it illustrates or adds to the discussion.

> **Key quote**
>
> 'Divine truth has to be refracted and expressed in terms of human words and finite images.'
>
> (Colin Brown)

> **Key quote**
>
> 'The qualifier "infinite" is a directive stimulating us to go on … and on … and on … until it dawns on us that when we talk of God we are not talking of something which is comparatively superior. Rather, it is that which evokes adoration, wonder, worship, commitment.'
>
> (Ian Ramsey)

> **Now test yourself**   Tested ☐
>
> 9   What are the two types of analogy that Aquinas identified?
>
> **Answer on page 108**

Symbolic   Revised ☐

A symbol has deep communicative power and evokes participation in the intended meaning (as opposed to a 'sign', which impacts on the intellect only). Common religious symbols include light and darkness.

Paul Tillich (1885–1965) argued that 'God-talk' is symbolic and cannot therefore be translated into literal assertions. Religious language that does not appear to be symbolic is actually symbolic. For instance, Tillich defined God as 'that which concerns us ultimately', or 'the ground of our being'. Hence, God is not 'a being' (who may or may not exist) but 'being' itself. This understanding of religious language as symbolic involves a total reinterpretation of the understanding of 'God'.

> **Key quote**
>
> 'Symbolic language alone is able to express the ultimate because it transcends the capacity of any finite reality to express it directly.'
>
> (Paul Tillich)

Myths

The **myth** is the most complex form of symbolic language. To many people, to speak of myths is to say something is untrue. However, the symbolic language of myths needs to be deciphered as myths are often associated with rite-of-passage events and seek to provide insights about our own existence, including origins.

> **Myth** – a symbolic story that tries to explain a fundamental issue about the purpose of existence.

Language games

The 'problems' of religious language disappear when it is no longer about things that are beyond experience. Indeed, according to some, religion does not involve some external being but our own psychology and feelings. This view would understand the phrase 'eternal life' as referring to the quality of life we should be experiencing now rather than anything to do with living forever.

These ideas about language being functional rather than illustrating information are based, in part, on the later work of Ludwig Wittgenstein. In his earlier work, Wittgenstein had influenced the Vienna Circle with his 'picture theory of language' (see page 60), but he later re-examined the question of meaning and concluded that words only have meaning because of their context. He referred to this approach as 'language games'. It was vital to know which context or 'game' one was playing. Wittgenstein used the example of the word 'soul'. He argued that problems are caused by trying to see the soul as some sort of physical object. The problems with religious language would dissolve if it was realised that the 'physical object' game simply does not apply to the soul.

Meaning emerges in the context of human activity, not from dependence on correspondence between word and object. Meaning is about convention and applying the word in the right way.

> **Key quotes**
>
> 'Don't ask for the meaning, ask for the use.'
>
> (Ludwig Wittgenstein)
>
> 'Philosophical problems arise when language goes on holiday.'
>
> (Ludwig Wittgenstein)
>
> 'Meaningfulness of discourse is determined by language users not by reality.'
>
> (Felicity McCutcheon)

Now test yourself

Tested

10 Explain the difference between Wittgenstein's picture theory of language and his later view of language as language games.

Answer on page 108

Religious language as non-cognitive

The table below illustrates the differences between cognitive and non-cognitive language.

Cognitive language	Non-cognitive language
Language refers – it illustrates information. For example, Jesus was born in Bethlehem.	Language is use – it is functional. For example, God is a rock.
Religious language is taken to be a method of referring as accurately as possible to the external reality of God	Religious language does not refer to reality, but is the medium in which reality is expressed.
Judgement on the meaning of religious language comes from surveys and literature of what believers take their beliefs to mean, for example, teaching by the Church.	Judgement on the meaning of religious language comes from examining the words of religion in their worshipping context, for example, 'God loves us'.

Issues arising

The main issues arising involve assessing the various approaches to religious language.

How successfully has religion responded to the challenges of these two principles?

Revised

The verification principle

The challenge to religion of the verification principle (VP) is the claim that God-talk is meaningless.

Response to challenge	Is response successful?

• God-talk is meaningless if it is taken to be cognitive. However, that is to misunderstand religious language. Religious language is non-cognitive and so the VP is irrelevant.
• The verification principle does not show that religious language is meaningless since verification is possible:
  – Eschatological verification possible.
  – Historical statements meaningful, for example, 'Jesus was raised from the dead'.
  – God is able to verify his own existence.
• The verification principle is flawed as it cannot itself be verified. There is no sense experience that can count in its favour.
	• Depends if you think religious language is non-cognitive. For example, is God a being that has properties or is God a term for 'being' itself?
	• Weak verification may be possible but is all religious language cognitive, for example, 'God is a rock'? If not, then how do you decide which are and which are not literal?
	• Could the experiences of resurrected beings verify God – or would the afterlife also be ambiguous?
	• Depends if you think experiences are subjective. If so, then the criterion for meaning is subjective and not, as logical positivists claimed, objective.
	• Depends if you think the picture theory of language is correct or whether religious language is more about function and use.

The falsification principle

The falsification principle (FP) raises questions about the status of religious statements. Others would go further and claim that it shows that religious language is meaningless.

If religious language is seen as cognitive, then the falsification principle can be challenged on the following grounds:

- Some non-falsifiable events are clearly meaningful, for example, toys that come out at night only when they cannot be detected. Because this statement cannot be falsified it is deemed meaningless *but we do* understand what the statement means and so it suggests the falsification test for meaningfulness is flawed.

- God's reality is different to physical objects and therefore the science paradigm of testing by falsification is inappropriate.

- The falsification principle fails its own test, since it is not clear what would count as evidence against the principle.

If religious language is seen as non-cognitive, then the *University* debate would reflect this view and the falsification principle would be irrelevant. However, many might feel that the non-cognitive approach is not without problems. For example, it is charged with not depicting reality and developing its own unique criteria of meaning and truth. Many religious claims are claims that are believed to be true for everyone, for example, the claim made by some believers that in Christianity Jesus died in order to bring salvation.

> **Exam tip**
>
> The issues arising are questions that test evaluation skills and are **not** about listing criticisms. They involve weighing up the relative strengths and weaknesses of those criticisms.

> **Typical mistake**
>
> Don't just learn a list of succinct key points or phrases. Remember that revision points are *reminders* of key areas and you need to develop them rather than recite them.

Exam practice answers at **www.therevisionbutton.co.uk/myrevisionnotes**

Additionally, it is difficult to decide whether a symbol can successfully represent something beyond our experience. There seems to be no way to judge whether a symbol is adequate. Neither is there any way to determine whether a symbol gives the correct insights about the ultimate.

Typical mistake

Don't recycle your answers to past questions; each question, even though they may sound similar, will have a different focus to ones you've used for practice.

Is it possible to talk meaningfully about God?   Revised

There are a number of ways of approaching this issue, including from an atheist/faith perspective and from a cognitive/non-cognitive debate.

Supporting arguments include:	Arguments against include:
• Refutation of the verification/falsification principles and arguing that religious language can be cognitive and meaningful.	• The verification/falsification principles show that religious language is meaningless.
• Religious statements are open to weak verification and so are meaningful (for example, eschatological verification).	• Non-cognitive understanding of religious language can reduce God-talk to expressions about attitudes to life rather than being about a personal being.
• Religious language is non-cognitive and therefore meaningful.	• Religious language is seen as an expression of our psychology (for example, Freud and Jung's explanations of religion in terms of psychology).
• God guides human beings to a true understanding.	

Now test yourself   Tested

11 State two weaknesses of the verification principle.
12 State two weaknesses of the falsification principle.
13 Give a criticism of the view that religious language is symbolic.

Answers on page 108

How successful are the various explanations of the nature of religious language?   Revised

This issue involves revisiting the arguments for and against the different understandings of religious language (cognitive and non-cognitive). These arguments are given on page 65 and their various strengths and weaknesses would need to be assessed.

Exam practice

(a) Explain how the following have challenged religious language:
   (i)   the verification principle
   (ii) the falsification principle.   **(30 marks)**
(b) To what extent is it possible to talk meaningfully about God?
                                       (20 marks)

Answers online   Online

3 Body, soul and personal identity

The soul

Human beings appear to be characterised by both body (physical) and mind (consciousness) properties. The body has physical properties such as height. My height is a fact. But I can also think about my height. At times I am self-conscious. The problem is whether mind and body are one and the same nature (**materialism**) or whether we have two natures (**dualism**).

> **Materialism** – the philosophy that everything human can be explained in empirical terms.
>
> **Dualism** – a fundamental twofold distinction, such as body and soul.

Nature
Revised ☐

There are a variety of views about the nature of the soul, including the soul as:

- **incorporeal**
- the immortal essence of a person
- capable of union with the divine
- created or uncreated
- Aristotle's idea that the soul was not a distinct substance from the body and that the soul is closer to the idea of a life force
- Aquinas' understanding of the soul as the *anima* because it was that which animated the body and gave it life.

> **Incorporeal** – without material form.

> **Key quote**
>
> '... the soul does not exist without a body and yet is not itself a kind of body. For it is not a body, but something which belongs to a body, and for this reason exists in a body, and in a body of such-and-such a kind.'
>
> (Aristotle)

Existence
Revised ☐

Plato's arguments

1 The 'use' argument

- A user differs from what is used.
- A human being uses his/her body.
- Therefore a human being must be different from the body.
- A person is either a body or soul. Therefore, a person must be a soul.

2 The 'recollection' argument

- We know with certainty that things in the world of the senses are not perfect – for example, we know beautiful things are not absolutely beautiful.
- We could not have this certainty if we did not already know what absolute beauty is.
- Therefore we must know absolute beauty innately.
- Therefore we must have lived before birth.

3 The 'opposites' argument

- In nature we observe cycles of opposites. Hot things become cold, and then cold things can become hot; living things die, and then life emerges from dead things, and so on.
- Therefore it is reasonable to suppose that when we die, we will be transformed into something alive.

Other arguments for the existence of the soul

Both the belief in **resurrection** and certain forms of reincarnation require the existence of the soul, because the soul is what allows us to maintain our identity in a *post-mortem* existence.

> **Resurrection** – coming back to life from the dead.

Exam practice answers at **www.therevisionbutton.co.uk/myrevisionnotes**

The body/soul relationship

Dualism

Dualists argue that people have composite natures, material and non-material. The non-material element is usually called the soul, spirit or mind. Many argue that the soul and mind are different; the soul represents the spiritual aspect of human beings, while the mind is more closely linked to the brain and related to reasoning.

As regards the inter-relationship of the body and mind, Descartes favoured interactionism, that is, the mind and body can interact. He concluded that the place of interaction was the brain and, in particular, in the pineal gland.

Even if there are two natures, it could well be that both perish at death. It would be odd that one should be mortal and the other immortal, given their interaction. Alternatively, one may argue it would be odd not to consider that one might survive death, given two natures of very different kinds.

Epiphenomenalism (another form of dualism) favours the view that bodily events can cause mental events. However, mental events cannot cause physical events. Therefore, at death both the physical and mental would cease.

> **Dualist** – someone who believes that the mind (soul) and body are separate entities.

Materialism

This view argues that so-called mental events are physical events occurring to physical objects. Gilbert Ryle (1900–1976) famously attacked dualism by calling Descartes' model 'the ghost in the machine'. The 'ghost' is the mind and the 'machine' is the body. Ryle rejected the idea of the mind as a different kind of thing from the body. He called it a **category mistake** – the brain and mind belong to different logical categories, which had been wrongly associated.

Ryle clarified this with an example of a foreigner visiting Oxford or Cambridge for the first time. On being shown a number of colleges, libraries and offices, they ask 'But where is the university?' The mistake was allocating the university to the same category as that to which the other various buildings belong. The university is not a separate entity and in a similar way, neither is the mind.

Those who favour materialism have often argued for a **replica theory** approach where the whole person is recreated after death (see page 71).

> **Category mistake** – the mistake committed when an object or concept that belongs in one category is treated as if it belongs in a category of a different logical type.
>
> **Replica theory** – John Hick's idea that God can instantaneously replicate someone at death into a new existence, despite the old mind and body perishing.

Now test yourself

1 List four views about the nature of the soul.
2 List three arguments cited by Plato (c.428–347BCE) to show the existence of the soul.
3 What is the difference between dualism and materialism in connection with the body/soul relationship debate?

Answers on page 108

> **Typical mistake**
>
> The view and argument are required in an exam answer. Biographical details are usually irrelevant. Stay focused.

Personal identity and life after death

Personal identity
Revised

Personal identity poses two important issues about personal existence after death:

- What criteria are there for deciding what constitutes a person? Can these be isolated and identified?
- What is the criterion necessary for somebody to be regarded as the same person?

It is possible to examine whether the characteristic that is isolated is the essential ingredient that makes a person a person:

Body	There is continuity though it is accepted that it changes with time. Resurrection and reincarnation do not have bodily continuity.
Memory	A unique aspect of each individual. But do you need physical characteristics to verify memory? Are we not more than the sum total of our memories?
Brain	The brain decays at death. Would it be a replica?
Personality	People have multiple personalities. Which is the 'real' person?
Personhood	Perhaps the 'I' is flexible and consists of a number of things, such as rational thought, consciousness, self-consciousness and emotions.
Soul	Similar to personhood but with the addition of freedom, moral responsibility and relationship to God.
Non-owner	'I' does not refer to anything apart from a stream of experiences that 'I' is supposed to own.

The various forms suggested will need to consider the question of personal identity.

Immortality
Revised

Immortality can be defined in several ways, but is ordinarily understood as the human soul surviving death, continuing in the possession of an endless conscious existence. This is a dualist view of the body and mind. Plato believed the soul belonged to a higher realm and was imperishable. He argued the body was a tomb or prison of the soul. The aim was to break free from physical matter so that the soul was free to go to the spiritual realm of true reality. Here it would be able to contemplate the true, the good and the beautiful. This idea is inherent in reincarnation, where the aim of the soul is ultimately to be absorbed into the oneness of God.

The philosopher Immanuel Kant believed that the purpose of existence was to achieve complete good (*summum bonum*), which was only possible if the soul was immortal, since the *summum bonum* could not be achieved in one lifetime. Most Christians accept the idea of an immortal soul that survives death.

> **Key quote**
>
> 'Our soul is of a nature entirely independent of the body, and consequently … it is not bound to die with it. And since we cannot see other causes which destroy the soul, we are naturally led to conclude that it is immortal.'
>
> (Descartes)

> **Exam tip**
>
> Remember that material studied in one part of the course can be drawn on to support an answer in another part – in particular, religious language that is concerned with the meaning of religious words.

Exam practice answers at **www.therevisionbutton.co.uk/myrevisionnotes**

Resurrection

Revised

The resurrection of the dead is a basic Christian belief. Traditionally, Christianity has held a dualist view with the mind/soul surviving death and being clothed in a new body. The New Testament gives an indication of the form of the resurrected body, if we regard Jesus' resurrection as a prototype. It could be touched and bore resemblance to the earthly body (Luke 24:39), yet at times it was not recognisable (Luke 24:13–32). It could also pass through matter (John 20:19) and disappear (Luke 24:51).

Some do not regard Jesus' resurrected body as the final spiritual body. John 20:17 suggests the ascended body was different. Paul describes the spiritual body in 1 Corinthians 15. However, if Christians are in a physical, resurrected state and physical environment, where will it be and what will they do?

A recent trend in Christian theology is to regard a human being as a psycho-physical unity. This raises problems about the nature of resurrection – particularly about personal identity, since the body/mind would cease to be at death. One solution is the philosopher John Hick's replica theory (see below). An alternative would be to argue that the individual continues to exist in the mind of God between death and resurrection.

Key quote

'The body that is sown is perishable, it is raised imperishable … it is sown a natural body, it is raised a spiritual body.'

(1 Corinthians 15:42–44)

Replica theory

Revised

John Hick argues from a materialist point of view. He presents three scenarios in which it is meaningful to call it the same person if someone dies and appears in a new world with the same memories, and so on. He uses the word 'replica' in inverted commas because he uses it in a particular sense – it is not logically possible for the original and the 'replica' to exist simultaneously, or for there to be more than one 'replica' of the same original.

The three scenarios are:

Scenario	Description
1 Someone suddenly ceases to exist in a certain place in this world and the next instant comes into existence in another place.	The person is exactly the same in both bodily and mental characteristics as the one who disappeared. There is continuity in memory and bodily characteristics as well as beliefs and habits. They would be conscious but not understand how they have now come to be in a different place.
2 The person dies and a 'replica' appears in another country.	Just as above, the same bodily and mental characteristics are present.
3 The person dies and reappears in a different world.	Again, the person has the same bodily and mental characteristics.

Hick maintains that in each of these three progressive examples, it is valid to say that it is the same person. For Hick, a person is an indissoluble psycho-physical unity and therefore the body is a necessity. Philosophers such as Terence Penelhum do not agree with Hick. The lack of bodily continuity questions whether it is correct to call the two people the same person.

Rebirth

Revised ☐

Buddhism teaches that there is an ever-changing character, which moves from **rebirth** to rebirth. It is neither a soul nor a fixed entity that is reborn – an evolving consciousness or a stream of consciousness would be more accurate. However, while there is continuity between each life, the consciousness in the new person is neither identical nor entirely different from that in the deceased. The two form a causal continuum or stream. Buddhism teaches that a person is made up of thoughts, feelings and perceptions interacting with the body in a dynamic and constantly changing way. Hence, all is impermanence.

It is much debated whether something that is ever-changing can be associated with personal identity and a personal *post-mortem* existence. It could be argued that we all undergo changes in our lives yet we remain recognisable as the same person. Therefore, the idea of a dynamic personality does not necessarily contradict the idea of identity.

> **Rebirth** – the Buddhist idea that energies are transferred from one existence to another.

Reincarnation

Revised ☐

In every body there is an 'atman' or soul that animates the body. Hindus believe the soul is eternal. Reincarnation involves the idea of transmigration of the soul from body to body. The 'I' who is now conscious has lived before, and will live again in other bodies. It involves a different body and no guarantee or need to remember past lives. The ultimate goal is to achieve release from the cycle of life, death and reincarnation and be reunited with Brahman (ultimate, absolute reality or universal soul): to lose personal identity.

The soul's place in life reflects the law of **karma**. Each action has a consequence. There is good karma (living in the right way according to the faith) and bad karma (disregarding the teachings of the faith). The consequences of an action may not be experienced in this life but influence events in the next life.

Clearly problems arise in regards to personal identity. Is it just that a person suffers now for sins committed in a previous life by a different person? Evidence to support reincarnation centres on supposed remembered lives. This implies a continuation of consciousness from one life to the next. In this view, it could be argued that reincarnation does support the idea of personal identity.

> **Karma** – actions or deeds that bring positive or negative results upon oneself, either in this life or in a reincarnation.

Key quote

'Just as a man discards worn out clothes and puts on new clothes, the soul discards worn out bodies and wears new ones.'

(Bhagavad Gita)

Now test yourself

4 Explain the difference between:
   (a) 'resurrection' and 'reincarnation'
   (b) 'reincarnation' and 'rebirth'.
5 What problem does the 'replica' theory seek to resolve?
6 Give one argument to support the idea of:
   (a) resurrection
   (b) reincarnation.

Answers on page 108

Exam tip

It is important at this level to use appropriate technical language. Be careful not to confuse the similar terms of resurrection, reincarnation and rebirth.

Near death experiences (NDEs)

Both near death experiences and out-of-body experiences involve a subject observing things from a point located outside their physical body. However, people who have NDEs consistently speak of meeting a 'being' of light and are often affected spiritually. The British psychiatrist Peter Fenwick (b. 1935) argues that NDEs have similar characteristics to mystical experiences.

Nature

Revised ☐

Raymond Moody (b. 1944), a philosopher and psychiatrist, coined the term NDE and brought NDEs to the attention of the public in his bestselling book *Life After Life* (Bantam, 1975). Later, Fenwick identified twelve features that describe a 'complete' experience, though he was not claiming that all twelve occurred in every NDE. The list comprises:

- feelings of peace
- out of body
- into the tunnel
- approaching the light
- the being of light
- the barrier
- another country
- meeting relatives
- the life review
- the point of decision
- the return
- the aftermath.

Others identify five 'stages': peace, body separation, entering the darkness (tunnel), seeing the light, and entering the light.

Key quote

'The NDE subject feels that he has seen through the very texture of the universe into its ultimate structure.'

(Peter Fenwick)

Typical mistake

Accounts of NDEs are useful as illustrations of features, but you need to allude to the accounts and comment on them in the light of the focus, rather than just give lengthy descriptions.

Value as evidence of survival beyond death

Revised ☐

An NDE seems to be a spiritual experience for most people. It is accompanied by a sensation of transcending space and time, of feelings of joy and peace, and positive changes in attitude and behaviour. In addition, the 'radiant and glowing' figure at the end of the tunnel experience is often associated in the mind of the subject with a spiritual being such as God, Jesus or Allah.

The appearance of 'otherworld journey' narratives occurs in most cultures and in the traditions of a number of world religions. The frequency of the accounts, their common features across cultures and the strength of the testimony gives strong support to life after death. In particular, the features of the accounts imply survival beyond death:

- soul–body dualism – there is an aspect of a person (their consciousness and physical senses) that exists separately from the body. This suggests that though the body may die there is something else that continues and which encapsulates personal identity.

- a spiritual realm/presence, indicated by the 'figures of light' – this suggests another realm after death exists in which life is lived, albeit in a different form. The person has clinically died yet they have a consciousness and an experience of travelling to a new existence.

- judgement – a review of the person's life is often cited as part of the experience – this suggests some continuity between this life and the life after death.

Key quotes

'I know a man in Christ who fourteen years ago was caught up to the third heaven … whether in the body or apart from the body I do not know, but God knows – was caught up to paradise. He heard inexpressible things …'

(2 Corinthians 12:2–4)

'O nobly-born, when thy body and mind were separating, thou must have experienced a glimpse of the Pure Truth, subtle, sparkling, bright, dazzling, glorious and radiantly awesome, in appearance like a mirage moving across a landscape in spring-time in one continuous stream of vibrations.'

(The Tibetan Book of the Dead)

Exam tip

Be careful when using quotes. Make sure you explain the relevance of the quote.

Now test yourself

Tested ☐

7   Explain how each of these people are connected with NDEs:
    (a) Raymond Moody
    (b) Peter Fenwick.

8   State and explain three features of NDEs that imply survival beyond death.

Answers on page 108

Issues arising

Is the notion of personal *post-mortem* existence coherent?

Revised ☐

The different views on life after death raise different philosophical problems about the coherency of the concept of a post-mortem existence. For instance:

● Is the concept meaningful?

To what extent does linguistic philosophy challenge the concept of life after death? Is it a contradictory concept?

● Continuity

If nothing continues after death, then in what sense can one say that it is the 'same' person after death? To what extent does the problem of continuity challenge the concept of life after death?

● Identification

To what extent are bodily criteria required as the means by which we recognise people?

● What kind of life is it?

What problems arise if the post-mortem world is a physical environment? What problems arise if the post-mortem world is not a physical environment?

Below are some arguments for and against the view that the post-mortem world is a coherent notion.

No	Yes
'Surviving death' is a meaningless phrase. It is self-contradictory.	A dualist could argue that you could witness your own funeral, since you are witnessing your body, an empty shell, not 'you'.
Materialism means that nothing can continue through death.	God could recreate us after death.
A replica means that nothing survives of the original entity. Therefore it is not the same person.	A replica is the same as the original, like a chalk message that can be erased and then rewritten.
There is no evidence. For example, some mediums have been shown to be frauds, some ghost sightings have been hoaxes, and other phenomena have some sort of natural explanation such as energy fields.	Evidence of personal *post-mortem* existence: ● spiritualism ● ghost sightings ● NDEs. Natural explanations and fraud/hoaxes account for some instances; some remain unexplained.
● *Post-mortem* life is either bodied or disembodied. ● If bodied, what type of body and would others recognise it as you? What is the 'I' that continues through death? ● If disembodied, would it be a dream world? Would we each create our own mental image world? This would be governed by the laws of psychology rather than those of physics. ● Both views of the post-mortem world are incoherent.	● St Paul likens the relationship of the earthly, physical body to the spiritual body using the analogy of the seed to the full-grown plant (1 Corinthians 15). ● Reported NDEs display the concept of selfhood applied to something other than the body. ● NDEs also suggest physical abilities through mental states, for example, seeing and hearing.

Do NDEs provide reasonable grounds for belief in the afterlife?

NDEs have often been used as evidence for the afterlife. Below is a table raising some questions about the evidence and the extent to which it is persuasive. Remember that AO2 questions are evaluative and so the conclusion must be reached by reasoned and justified arguments.

Criticisms that question the validity of NDEs	Persuasive?
In medieval accounts of NDEs, entering the tunnel is replaced by sailing in a ship. This suggests NDEs are based on culture and imagination.	Cultural differences might help a person understand what is happening, rather than imagination. Do reports of NDEs in every age and culture strengthen or weaken the case?
Modern-day understanding tends to reject a dualistic view of human beings. The mind cannot be separated from the physical body.	What about extra-sensory perception? That would support dualism.
The experience is near death – not at death or after death. Therefore, the experience cannot convey what happens after death.	The people are often judged clinically dead. Does the fact that they survive death deny the experience?
That the person is usually a patient in hospital and on medication suggests that drugs may be the cause of the experience.	This doesn't account for all NDEs. Would different drugs still produce the same core characteristics of NDEs?
Oxygen deprivation can produce similar effects to an NDE. Recent research shows changes in the visual cortex can produce a tunnel effect with white light at the end.	Surely this would affect the clarity of the memory? Are all aspects of the experience explained by oxygen deprivation?
Carl Sagan argued that at the point of death the memory of birth is relived and hence the tunnel is likened to the birth canal, the white light – the light of the world as you are born, and the being of light – the midwife attending at birth.	Is the brain developed enough in newborn babies to be able to perceive objects? Why do those born by Caesarean have similar NDEs? The baby's face is usually pressed against the wall of the birth canal so why would it have the sensation of travelling towards light?
Hearing is the last sense to be lost, so accurate accounts of being resuscitated may be the memory of what they hear going on around them. It is likely that many people, when dying, will imagine the world they expect or hope to see. Their minds may turn to people they have known who have died before them.	A number of NDEs experienced by children under seven have been reported. They describe vivid events, people and places with words and knowledge that are beyond their years. They do not expect to die and have not been exposed to cultural or religious views. Could it be inherited memory or evidence of life after death?

The different explanations tend to focus only on parts of the experience. Does it require an overall explanation of the whole experience to prove NDEs are evidence of an afterlife?

Is the notion of the soul coherent?

You should consider the dualistic view and the materialistic view of the soul. The following questions may help:

● How can a non-physical soul influence or be influenced by the physical body?

● Is the idea of a soul meaningful? How could it be verified or falsified?

● If souls were unattached to bodies then what would form boundaries between them? Would they just mould into one?

● Does it make sense to think that our personal identity can be encapsulated in the notion of a soul? What exactly would the soul be?

Are there reasonable grounds for belief in the existence of a soul?

You should weigh up actual evidence for the existence of a soul rather than just concepts about the soul. The following questions may help:

● How persuasive are Plato's arguments for the existence of the soul?

● Is Ryle right when he talks of the soul as a 'category mistake'?

● Is the evidence for dualism persuasive?

● How convincing is the evidence for the various accounts of survival after death, for example, resurrection, reincarnation, rebirth, NDEs?

● To what extent do these different accounts of survival after death support the idea of a soul?

● What would constitute 'reasonable grounds'?

> **Typical mistake**
>
> Remember, your conclusion may decide that there is no clear conclusion. Both sides have equal strengths and weaknesses. However, any conclusion reached must be justified from what has been argued in the rest of the answer.

Now test yourself

Tested

9 Do differences in medieval accounts of NDEs mean that NDE accounts are to be explained as the product of imagination? Justify your answer.

10 Why might accounts of NDEs by children suggest that NDEs are genuine?

Answers on page 108

Exam practice

(a) Analyse what is meant by a near death experience. **(30 marks)**

(b) To what extent does a near death experience prove there is survival after death? **(20 marks)**

Answers online

Online

4 The problem of evil

The concept of evil

The notion of evil can cover everything that is harmful and destructive in the world, so it is very difficult to give a clear, concise definition. The philosopher David Hume conveys the sense of the term: 'a hospital full of disease, a prison crowded with malefactors and debtors, a field of battle strewed with carcasses, a fleet foundering in the ocean, a nation languishing under tyranny, famine, or pestilence' (*Dialogues Concerning Natural Religion*, Bobbs-Merrill Educational Publishing, 1970 (first published 1779)).

Other ideas include the physical state of pain, the mental states of suffering and the experience of injustice. Philosophy tends to classify evil into two broad categories: moral and natural.

Moral evil   Revised ☐

Moral evils are events in which responsible actions cause suffering or harm, for example, murder, stealing or lying. They are the result of a person who is morally blameworthy and intended their actions.

Natural evil   Revised ☐

This is seen in events such as earthquakes and diseases, which cause suffering but over which human beings have little or no control. Certain events have been used as classic illustrations of natural evil. At one stage it was the Lisbon earthquake of 1755, but in the present day it could be the tsunami of 2004, the Haiti earthquake of 2010, or the rise of AIDS and cancer.

> **Key quote**
>
> 'Nearly all the things which men are hanged or imprisoned for doing to one another, are Nature's everyday performances.'
>
> (J S Mill (1806–1873))

The logical problem of evil   Revised ☐

The logical problem of evil was first formulated by the Greek philosopher Epicurus (343–270BCE). If we accept that God is both all-powerful and all-good, then the assumption is that a good God would eliminate evil as far as he is able. Why does the God who has the power to eliminate all evil not do so? God has the means (power) and the motivation (love, goodness) to eliminate evil but chooses not to.

As an argument:

- God is all-powerful.
- God is all-good.
- God opposes evil.
- Therefore, evil does not exist in the world.

Exam practice answers at **www.therevisionbutton.co.uk/myrevisionnotes**

A theist would agree with the premises, yet would not agree with the conclusion.

A possible response is to challenge the notion of **omnipotence** by arguing that God cannot do that which is logically impossible – create free agents who can do only what is good. This type of individual **free will** is incompatible with **determinism**. However, natural evil remains difficult to explain (see section on the free-will defence, page 80).

Omnipotence – the power to do anything; to be all-powerful. Some philosophers exclude the logically impossible.

Free will – the ability to make choices that are not determined by prior causes or by divine intervention.

Determinism – for everything that happens there are conditions such that, given those conditions, nothing else could happen.

Key quote

'Either God cannot abolish evil, or he will not; if he cannot then he is not all-powerful; if he will not then he is not all-good.'

(Augustine)

The evidential problem of evil
Revised

This is an **inductive** argument in that it attempts to demonstrate that the existence of evil in the world counts against the claim that God exists:

- There exist instances of intense suffering.
- An all-powerful, all-good God would prevent the occurrence of any intense suffering (omnipotence includes **omniscience**).
- Therefore, there does not exist an all-powerful, all-good being.

The evidential argument is a matter of weighing up probabilities. Given the evidence of suffering, which is the most likely – that there is a God, or that there is no God and the world is indifferent?

Inductive – a process of reasoning that draws a general conclusion from specific instances.

Omniscience – the characteristic of being all-knowing.

Now test yourself
Tested

1 What is the difference between the logical problem of evil and the evidential problem of evil?
2 Explain why some people argue that God could not create free agents who can only do what is good.

Answers on page 108

Typical mistake

It is not enough to say that God is all-powerful and all-loving and therefore the existence of evil causes a problem. You need to spell out why those attributes of God – power and love – are seen as inconsistent with evil existing.

Religious responses

The religious responses to the problem of evil have been in the form of theodicies. A **theodicy** is an attempt to solve the problem of evil by showing that God is justified in allowing evil. It usually takes the form of giving a good reason or set of reasons for God not preventing or eliminating evil. Four of the main theodicies are discussed on the following pages.

Theodicy – a justification of the righteousness of God, given the existence of evil.

1 Augustinian theodicies

The philosopher Augustine (354–430CE) approached the problem of evil from a variety of angles but did not fully define it. The Augustinian-type theodicies reflect the traditional Christian approach. The main themes are as follows:

> **Ex nihilo** – a Latin phrase meaning 'out of nothing', that is, God did not use any previously existing materials when he created.

- God created out of nothing (**ex nihilo**).
- Creation is good.
- Human beings were created perfect.
- Human beings have free will.
- Human beings used their free will to turn away from God (the Fall).

- The Fall ushered into the world both moral and natural evil.
- God foresaw, from the foundation of the world, the Fall of human beings and planned their redemption through Christ.
- God made repentance and salvation possible.

As God is the author of everything in the created universe, evil is not a substance, otherwise it would mean God created it. For Augustine, evil is a privation. A privation is the absence or lack of something that ought to be there. It is the malfunctioning of something that in itself is good.

The emphasis of this theodicy is **soul-deciding**. Our response to evil and God's rescue plan of salvation (belief in Jesus Christ and his death for us) determines what happens to us when we die.

> **Soul-deciding** – people's response to evil decides their destiny (Augustinian-type theodicy).

2 The free-will defence

Free will is implicit in the Augustinian-type theodicy (see above). It is argued that the evil that exists in the world is due to humanity's misuse of the gift of free will. God created a world in which human beings could decide freely to love and obey God.

> **Soul-making** – the presence of evil helps people to grow and develop (Hick's theodicy).

In John Hick's 'vale of **soul-making**' theodicy (see page 81) the world is seen as a 'vale of soul-making'. Through suffering, human souls are made nobler so suffering is seen as of benefit to humanity. People have freedom to come to God since God deliberately creates a world in which it is not immediately and overwhelmingly evident that there is a God. Hence human goodness occurs through making free and responsible moral choices, in situations of difficulty and temptation.

> **Typical mistake**
>
> A common mistake is to mix up the two classic theodicies. Although they have similarities, remember that the Augustinian is *from* perfection whereas the Irenaean/ Hick's is *to* perfection.

The philosopher Richard Swinburne (b. 1934) addressed the problem of the sheer quantity of evil, which many feel is unnecessarily large. He said a genuinely free person must be allowed to harm themselves and others. God could intervene or let them learn from the consequences. The latter is more in keeping with the exercise of moral freedom. God does not give human beings unlimited power to do harm, since death brings an end to suffering. According to Swinburne, 'the less God allows men to bring about large-scale horrors, the less the freedom and responsibility he gives them'. In other words, we can make real, significant, far-reaching choices.

> **Exam tip**
>
> Remember that some questions may not require a full account of the theodicy. Select those aspects of the theodicy that are relevant to the particular focus of the question. This demonstrates selection skills (AO1).

Now test yourself

Tested

3 Explain why the Augustinian traditional theodicy is called soul-deciding.

4 According to Swinburne, how does the free-will defence address the problem of the sheer quantity of evil?

Answers on page 108

3 The 'vale of soul-making' theodicy

Revised

The English theologian and philosopher John Hick developed a theodicy from his understanding of Irenaeus (130–202), an **Early Church Father** and Bishop of Lyon. Irenaeus wrote about the idea that human beings are developing towards perfection. Irenaeus made a distinction between the 'image' and the 'likeness' of God (Genesis 1:26). Adam had the form of God but not the content of God. Adam and Eve were expelled from the Garden of Eden because they were immature and needed to develop; they were to grow into the likeness (content) of God. They were the raw material for a further stage of God's creative work.

The Fall of humanity is seen as an inevitable part of humanity maturing. This happens as free persons make decisions about their lives and the world. John Hick took these ideas and developed them into a full theodicy:

- The first phase of God making humankind in his image was the culmination of the evolutionary process, whereby a creature evolved who had the possibility of existing in conscious fellowship with God.

- The second phase involved a being that makes moral responsible choices in real-life situations.

- God deliberately created a world in which it is not immediately and overwhelmingly evident that there is a God. This is called an **epistemic distance**.

- Human goodness that occurs through making free and responsible moral choices is more valuable than 'ready-made' goodness.

- Some moral goods are responses to evils and hence cannot exist without them – for example, compassion. These are called **second-order goods**.

- This process is worthwhile because of the eventual outcome. If the process is not completed in this life, then Hick argued we go to another life in another realm until the process is complete.

- Evil and suffering are justified since they are the means by which all human beings will eventually succeed in becoming morally perfect.

- The emphasis in this theodicy is on soul-making.

Early Church Father – term used of the early and influential theologians and writers in the Christian Church in the first five centuries of Christian history. It does not include the New Testament authors.

Epistemic distance – distance from knowledge of God – God is hidden and so allows human beings to choose freely.

Second-order goods – moral goods that are a response to evil.

Key quote

'[The value of this world] is to be judged, not primarily by the quantity of pleasure and pain occurring in it at any particular moment, but by its fitness for its primary purpose, the purpose of soul-making'.

(John Hick)

4 Process theodicy

The starting point of process theodicy is to question:

(a) the view that God is omnipotent

(b) the assumption that he is capable of destroying evil.

Its main proponents are A N Whitehead and David Griffin. The problem of evil is removed by redefining the meaning of omnipotence. The main ideas are:

- Creation was not *ex nihilo* but was the achievement of order out of pre-existing chaos.
- God's power is limited since the pre-existing materials are not totally subject to God's will.
- God is depicted not as a powerful almighty despot, but rather as a being that creates by persuasion and attempts to influence things into being.
- God is in time, and both affects and is affected by the world.
- God depends on his creatures to shape the course of his own experiences.
- God cannot control finite beings but can only set them goals that he then has to persuade them to actualise.
- Evil occurs when such goals are not realised.

This theodicy is a reaction against the classical Augustinian-type theodicies in which God seems unaffected by our suffering, this world and its experiences are seen as relatively unimportant, and we reach salvation by escaping from this realm. In contrast, process theodicy stresses life on Earth and maintains that the most real thing about a person is the series of experiences that make up the process of this life here and now. God is seen as intimately involved with this world and its suffering; indeed, God is called a 'co-sufferer'.

Now test yourself

 Tested

5 Why is the epistemic distance an important aspect of John Hick's theodicy?

6 Why is John Hick's theodicy called the 'vale of soul-making'?

7 In what way can process theodicy be seen as a reaction against the Augustinian-type theodicies?

Answers on page 108

Issues arising

The success of the theodicies as a response to the problem of evil

Revised

It is necessary to assess how successful the theodicies are in addressing the problem of evil and in justifying the existence of both moral and natural evil. The tables below give examples of both criticisms of and responses to the theodicies, and then raise some issues you may want to consider.

Augustinian-type theodicy

Criticisms	Responses	Success
1 The Fall depicted in Genesis contradicts evolutionary development.	The Fall is not literal but represents each person's rebellion against God.	Depends on the interpretation and authority of the Bible.
2 If God created perfect human beings who sinned, then they must have been created with a flaw.	It is not possible to simultaneously create free beings and make them always choose the good.	Jesus was human and never did wrong. So maybe it is possible?
3 God is responsible for evil since he chose to create a being he foresaw would do evil.	He set in place a rescue plan to redeem and save. It is better to create and experience love, than not to create at all.	Maybe God didn't know until human beings had enacted their free will? Does love outweigh the amount of suffering experienced?
4 The existence of hell is not consistent with a loving God.	People must be free to choose. Some argue for annihilation rather than hell.	Depends on view of existence of hell. Maybe all are saved?
5 Evil is not a privation/lack but a real entity.	Evil is an absence of good.	Depends on the devil's existence.
6 Since everything depends on God for its existence, is free will possible?	There is limited free will in that God's ultimate plans cannot be thwarted.	Depends on the role of God in the universe and on the view about the nature of free will.

Free-will defence

Criticisms	Responses	Success
1 God could have chosen to create a world without free creatures.	Such a world would have no value. Love demands freedom of choice.	Depends if a world without evil is better than a world with free creatures and evil in it.
2 God could have created beings who always choose the good.	It is not possible to simultaneously create free beings and make them always choose the good.	Jesus was human and never did wrong. So maybe it is possible?
3 There is no justification for natural evil.	Human evil has affected all of creation. Natural evil provides the epistemic distance.	Depends on which theodicy you link the free will defence to and whether it provides a convincing justification.

'Vale of soul-making'

Criticisms	Responses	Success
1 Does the end justify the means? Can the suffering experienced justify the ultimate joy?	All ultimately experience the joy and the joy lasts eternally.	Depends if you think the ends could be achieved without so much suffering.
2 Could not the greater goods be gained without such evil/suffering?	To show compassion, etc. requires the existence of evil.	Are the greater goods worth the pain and suffering?
3 Evil often ruins and destroys people rather than making them perfect.	Ultimately, all will achieve the goal of perfection.	Could not the end be achieved with less suffering?
4 As a Christian theodicy, the death of Jesus and forgiveness seem irrelevant.	Jesus' death is seen as an inspiring example.	Depends on your view of Jesus and what his death achieved.
5 There is no evidence for other lives after death.	There is evidence – for example, remembered lives, spiritualism.	Depends on how convincing you find the evidence.

Process theodicy

Criticisms	Responses	Success
1 God is not the God of **classical theism**.	Fits in with modern evolutionary theories.	Depends if you think the traditional view of God is correct.
2 There is no guarantee that good will ultimately overcome evil.	That is the nature of God and the universe.	Depends on view of the nature of God and the universe.
3 Is death the end?	There are no guarantees. Unknown.	Does it matter?
4 Is such a God worthy of worship?	Relationship to God is not about worship.	Depends on view of the nature of God.

Classical theism – the belief in a personal deity, creator of everything that exists, who is distinct from that creation and is sustainer and preserver of the universe.

Exam tip

Do not just give a list of criticisms like a shopping list. It is far better to discuss and develop three or four criticisms, explaining why they are criticisms and then responding to them, than to give a list of seven or eight. This demonstrates a process of reasoning and sustained argument (AO2).

Now test yourself

Tested ☐

8 'The existence of hell is not consistent with a God of love.' Give an argument against this view.

9 'The death of Jesus seems irrelevant in the "vale of soul-making" theodicy.' Explain why, and give an argument against this view.

10 **(a)** Explain why in process theodicy God is not seen as the God of classical theism.

(b) Explain why this view of God in process theodicy is not seen as a problem to many people.

Answers on page 109

What poses the greatest challenge to faith in God – natural evil or moral evil?

You need to weigh up the extent to which particular types of evil (natural/moral) seem contrary to the existence of an all-powerful and all-loving God.

Different theodicies offer different justifications. Process theodicy sees the origin of evil in the inherent chaos within uncreated matter. Moral evil is usually seen as the easiest to justify since its roots lie in the free actions of human beings and therefore exempt God from any responsibility. It is free will misused by human beings.

However:

- Why didn't God create beings that always freely choose to do right and so remain perfect?
- Where did the temptation to do evil come from if evil only existed after the decision was made?
- Is the concept of free will meaningful? It is not clear how decisions that are made can be totally free – surely they are the result of nature and nurture?
- How loving is God if he created human beings knowing the pain and suffering that would result?
- Surely God could intervene and reduce the amount of moral evil in the world?
- Doesn't free will contradict the idea of a God on whom everything depends for its existence?

These questions may suggest moral evil is a challenge to faith in God.

Natural evil does not seem clearly related to the free actions of human beings but is rather part of God's creation. It is part of our environment and causes pain and suffering, such as floods and disease. Therefore, God seems solely responsible.

However:

- Human beings are part of God's creation. Is it therefore possible that there is some connection between human beings and natural evil?
- If we were more in tune with God, might it be possible to avoid natural evil?
- Isn't natural evil only evil when it causes suffering or pain?
- Could natural evil be necessary to produce second-order goods?

These questions may suggest natural evil is **not** such a challenge to faith in God. The evaluation will involve assessing the relative strengths and weaknesses of answers to these and other questions.

Is free will a satisfactory explanation for the existence of evil in a world created by God?

Revised

Is free will a satisfactory explanation for the existence of evil in a world created by God? To answer this you need to focus on:

● the nature of free will and its implications for an all-powerful, all-loving God

● the different types of evil and the different problems that they pose

● the different justifications presented by the various theodicies that appeal to free will as an explanation for the existence of evil.

The strengths and weaknesses of these responses to the problem of evil

Revised

Some examples are listed below. The weaknesses are identified more fully in the table above that lists the criticisms made against the various theodicies. A few of the key ones are repeated below.

Theodicy	Strength	Weakness
Augustinian	Accepts authority of Scripture and the Genesis account. Evil not created by God. Natural evil explained.	Literal account of Genesis contrary to modern thinking. God responsible since he created beings he foresaw would do evil.
Free-will defence	God not responsible for evil.	God could have created free beings who always did good. Free will is not a meaningful concept.
Hick's 'vale of soul-making'	Consistent with modern thinking about origins of life. All evil is justified since ultimately all achieve the goal of heaven.	If end result is guaranteed, what is the point of the pilgrimage? As a Christian theodicy, it seems to make the death of Jesus unnecessary.
Process	Consistent with evolutionary theories. God is not distant but a co-sufferer. Removes the logical problem by denying God's omnipotence.	Radical departure from classical theism. No guarantee that good will ultimately overcome evil. The God depicted is not worthy of worship.

Now test yourself

Tested

11 Give two arguments that suggest that moral evil is a challenge to faith in God.

12 Give two arguments that suggest that natural evil is not a challenge to faith in God.

13 State one strength of each of the four theodicies that you have studied.

Answers on page 109

Exam practice

(a) Explain what is meant by the problem of evil. **(30 marks)**

(b) 'The "vale of soul-making" theodicy successfully answers the problem of evil.' Assess this claim. **(20 marks)**

Answers online

Online

Topic I Life, death and beyond

The nature and value of human life

Religious: Christianity

The nature of humanity in Christian teaching goes back to the Biblical story of how God created the world. Human beings were created from the earth and are physical entities; however, they also have a spiritual aspect, that is, a 'soul' or 'spirit'.

Human beings were also created in the 'image' and after the 'likeness' of God (Genesis 1:26). Although lower than angels and higher than animals, it is their ensoulment that brings uniqueness. Human life is a gift from God. In the creation stories of Genesis, human beings are clearly the pinnacle of God's creation and are given **dominion** of the planet.

Originally, human beings were created without sin but with **free will**. Adam and Eve disobeyed God, and through sin brought death and imperfection into the world. The relationship between humanity and God was broken. Some refer to this as 'the Fall' and it has been traditional Christian teaching that we were all present seminally in the sin of Adam so that we all inherit a sinful nature.

Despite this, part of the status of humanity, being the most cherished of God's creation, is that human beings can redeem themselves by accepting the grace and forgiveness of God through Jesus Christ (Son of God). Jesus became 'flesh' (**incarnation**), sufferered and died for sins only to be **resurrected** to re-establish the order of creation.

Secular

A non-religious perspective would highlight that since there is no creator God, human beings are not 'created beings'. Life has evolved over millions of years. The idea of a 'spiritual' aspect to humanity is rejected and non-religious views speak of a 'mind' and not a soul. Richard Dawkins' (b. 1941) quote is often referred to as an explanation of **materialism**, recognising the **holistic** nature of mind and body.

> **Dominion** – the idea that human beings are in control of the planet.
>
> **Free will** – the ability to make choices that are not determined by prior causes or by divine intervention.
>
> **Incarnation** – God becoming human, for example, Jesus.
>
> **Resurrected** – brought back to life from the dead.

> **Key quote**
>
> 'Let us make man in our image, in our likeness, and let them rule over the fish of the sea and the birds of the air, over the livestock, over all the earth, and over all the creatures that move along the ground.'
>
> (Genesis 1:26)

> **Key quote**
>
> 'There is no spirit-driven life force, no throbbing, heaving, pullulating, protoplasmic, mystic jelly. Life is just bytes and bytes and bytes of digital information.'
>
> (Richard Dawkins, *River out of Eden*, 1995)

> **Materialism** – the mind and body are integrated and both disintegrate at death, meaning there is no disembodied existence beyond death.
>
> **Holistic** – concerning something that deals with the 'whole' picture.

In his book, *What is Your Dangerous Idea?* (Simon and Schuster, 2006), the psychologist John Hogan discusses the 'search for the neural code' and points out that **materialist** thinkers are trying to demonstrate beyond all doubt that the idea of the soul is dead; in other words, that human beings are beyond question only mortal. There is research in modern psychology to pinpoint the physical origins of neurosis, almost like a DNA of the mind that originates with our physical properties. If such a code were discovered, then all need for a mystical soul, and consequently the notion of immortality, would be eradicated. In a follow-up paper, another scientist claimed that the death of the soul would have dramatic consequences for the world as we know it.

According to a scientific view, human beings are simply a species within the process of evolution, evolving into its own niche within the tapestry of life. Any hint of divine activity within this process is rejected as we are simply carriers of DNA. It is our genetic make-up or DNA that becomes the 'soul' of our lives. Our sense of self and individuality has its basis in digital information, in genes working together to give a sense of being human. Any ideas about a spiritual world beyond this one are sheer imagination. However, this does not eradicate responsibility for the environment – according to thinkers like Dawkins it should make us even more aware of our total responsibility for the world we inhabit. Since we are part and parcel of a major and complex ecosystem it is only right that we respect and care for other parts. To abuse this would be to potentially threaten or abuse our own futures.

> **Materialist** – to do with the philosophy that everything human can be explained in empirical terms.

Exam tip

Do not answer a question by simply giving a descriptive account. Your answer should always select the key events, that is, the appropriate information relevant to the question. This demonstrates more personal understanding or 'ownership' of the knowledge. It is evidence that 'information is mostly accurate and relevant' (AO1).

Typical mistake

Some candidates mistime their answers. Make sure that your timing is correct and you have enough time to answer the second section.

Now test yourself   Tested ☐

1   How are human beings different from the rest of creation according to Christianity?

2   What is the 'search for the neural code'?

3   How do materialists explain the notion of the 'soul'?

Answers on page 109

Eschatological and apocalyptic teaching

Different teachings

Revised

Eschatology is the term used to describe writings that deal with 'the end times' or the end of the world as we know it. 'Apocalypse' (άποκάλυψις) is a Greek word meaning 'revelation', literally an 'unveiling' or 'unfolding' of previously unknown information regarding the end times. **Apocalyptic** literature is writing that reveals the precise details of the end days.

Religious: Christianity

Such writings within religion appear to have common themes such as:

- dramatic depictions of significant signs or events
- the destruction of the world
- a battle between good and evil with good being triumphant
- a focus on the hardships and oppressions of the end times
- a focus on the intensifying evil of the end times
- a focus on the despair of humanity in the end times.

However, despite all the doom and gloom, the prophetic (apocalyptic) aspect often provides a future hope of salvation and often a 're-creation' of a new order. The visions are often enigmatic (with a hidden code to reveal) and full of imagery. The classic eschatological and apocalyptic writing is the book of Revelation in the Bible.

The book of Revelation has fascinated and puzzled Christians for centuries. With its vivid imagery of disaster and suffering – the Battle of Armageddon, the Four Horsemen of the Apocalypse, the hideous beast whose number is 666 – many have seen it as a map to the end of the world.

> **Eschatology** – religious teachings about the end days, for example, when God calls Judgement Day.
>
> **Apocalyptic** – religious writings that are prophetic in nature and reveal truths about the end days.

Key quote

'Then I saw another beast, coming out of the earth. He had two horns like a lamb, but he spoke like a dragon. He exercised all the authority of the first beast on his behalf, and made the earth and its inhabitants worship the first beast, whose fatal wound had been healed. And he performed great and miraculous signs, even causing fire to come down from heaven to earth in full view of men. Because of the signs he was given power to do on behalf of the first beast, he deceived the inhabitants of the earth. He ordered them to set up an image in honour of the beast that was wounded by the sword and yet lived. He was given power to give breath to the image of the first beast, so that it could speak and cause all who refused to worship the image to be killed. He also forced everyone, small and great, rich and poor, free and slave, to receive a mark on his right hand or on his forehead, so that no one could buy or sell unless he had the mark, which is the name of the beast or the number of his name.

This calls for wisdom. If anyone has insight, let him calculate the number of the beast, for it is man's number. His number is 666.'

(Revelation 13:11–18)

There have been many different interpretations of this Scripture from predicting global warming and AIDS to several natural and human-created disasters. Some Biblical scholars, studying the text alongside the social and political history of the time, have a different interpretation. They see it as the anger of John (the author) at the Roman Empire due to its persecution of early Christians. Some Christians today see natural disasters such as tsunamis as the consequence of sin damaging our environment and causing global warming. Some see such disasters as 'signs' of the end days.

Ultimately, while there are pessimistic depictions of the final days, the religious perspective is hopeful of a new, reborn existence that is much more optimistic.

Secular

End times or disaster scenarios are not exclusive to religion. Secular predictions afford the planet another 5 billion years at the most, at which point the sun will become unstable. Other concerns or 'predictions' include:

- a massive asteroid collision
- melting ice-caps and worldwide floods as a result of global warming
- world war
- unintentional side-effects of advanced experimentation, for example, biochemical or physics (CERN accelerator that measures and observes particle collision).

While secular thinking does not involve a 'beast' like religious imagery does, it could be argued that the end of the world is a result of human beings not caring and similarly behaving like destructive beasts. While human beings are potentially the cause for some of these scenarios, in all cases the ultimate fate of the universe is beyond human control, not in the hands of a divine entity.

Exam tip

Remember to explain each point that you make in an exam answer to the full. Think carefully about each sentence and how it relates to the question and the previous sentence. Aim for at least three sentences to explain a point. For example, state what the point is, how it is understood and then give an example. This will help to ensure 'a thorough treatment of the topic within the time available' (AO1).

Now test yourself

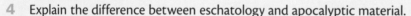

Tested ☐

4 Explain the difference between eschatology and apocalyptic material.
5 What are the main characteristics of eschatology and apocalyptic writings?

Answers on page 109

Typical mistake

Some candidates prepare for the exam only by learning answers to past questions. You need to be aware of the full specification.

Importance of the present life and life after death

Religious: Christianity

In essence, the purpose of human life is to worship and enjoy God with a view to continuing this relationship in heaven after death. This 'relationship' between God and humanity is seen in the Judaeo-Christian tradition through ideas of **covenant** and **chosen people**. In its infancy this relationship involved a betrayal and disobedience on the part of humanity; however, the purpose of humanity is to achieve its potential as sons and daughters of God through the new covenant established through Jesus Christ. Jesus' selfless act of suffering and dying for humanity means human beings must redeem themselves through the forgiveness that Jesus offers by his act of atonement. This eradicates any self-imposed punishments that may have been brought about through humanity's sinful nature.

> **Covenant** – an agreement between God and human beings.
> **Chosen people** – the belief that the Jewish people were exclusive to the covenant.

The practical outcome of this re-established relationship is to:

- worship God
- enjoy a relationship with God
- follow God's teachings as directed in the holy books
- maintain belief in Jesus as the Son of God.

The final goal is eternal salvation. Therefore the idea of this life and the next are inextricably linked and totally interdependent. This present life is the foundation of what is to come beyond death and so moral and religious behaviour are central to the religious teachings on how to live this life. Such teachings include the Ten Commandments (Exodus 20), and Jesus' teachings on law and behaviour, which can be summarised by the two quotes on the right.

Key quote

'"Love the Lord your God with all your heart and with all your soul and with all your strength and with all your mind"; and, "Love your neighbour as yourself."'

(Luke 10:27; known as the 'Greatest Commandment')

Some of the most influential teachings of Jesus can be found in the Sermon on the Mount. Jesus highlights the need for careful thought and reflection before an action and he also points out the hypocrisy of judging others who have done wrong when our own thoughts and failings prove that no one is perfect except God.

Key quote

'So in everything, do to others what you would have them do to you.'

(Matthew 7:12; known as the 'Golden Rule')

The New Testament portrays the notion of a Judgement Day 'in the presence of God and of Christ Jesus, who will judge the living and the dead' (2 Timothy 4:1). Both unbelievers and believers will be judged. However, for the believer, the judgement is not one of condemnation or death since 'there is now no condemnation for those who are in Christ Jesus' (Romans 8:1). The judgement is about bestowing various degrees of reward in the afterlife. Theologians point out that happiness is not based on the status or power that we have. For the Christian, happiness consists in delighting in God in this life on Earth.

Secular

Scientists such as Dawkins tend to reject the idea of **teleological** purpose, that is, the idea that the human race and life itself has a goal towards which it is working and which is driven from the beginning. The survival of the fittest is the purpose of humanity, if there is one, and is purely biological in explanation, not **metaphysical**. Life on Earth has no future purpose other than helping to determine the global evolution of the planet. Human beings are to express purpose in life through contributing to the whole.

Most religions seek an answer to life beyond life. For Dawkins, this is irrational as to think as a scientist and to reason based upon evidence is more appropriate. Despite not acknowledging a divine controller or a teleological end to life, non-religious people still see that human life has much value and potential.

The fact that human beings have evolved to the point of actually searching for meaning in life is wonderful in itself, creation **myth** apart. It is not relevant to worry about the meaning of the whole or human beings' place in the universe because they 'are' the universe. As human beings we have the greatest status and intellect on the planet and have the power to shape our own destiny as a species. Our genes manipulate on the biological level but it is our **memes** (memories of key ideas) from, for example, the sciences and arts, which develop us collectively as a species. Morality is not revealed to human beings by some divine being but worked out biologically through the whole process of evolution. This idea has a **utilitarian**-like appeal, which suits the majority.

Teleological – concerning the idea that there is a purpose to some thing or action that can be seen by looking at the outcome or end.

Metaphysical – to do with a non-physical realm.

Myth – a symbolic story that tries to explain a fundamental issue about the purpose of existence.

Memes – biologically generated memories that are transferred non-genetically through culture or behaviour.

Utilitarian – concerning the idea that the greatest good for the greatest number is the right course of action to take.

Now test yourself

Tested ☐

6 Why is the idea of a 'relationship with God' important for Christians?

7 Give three reasons why, according to Christians, the present life is important to the next life.

8 What evidence is there in life, according to secular thought, that part of us does live on in some form?

Answers on page 109

Exam tip

Make sure that you know all about religious and non-secular views because the distinction is often made in examination questions.

Typical mistake

Some candidates get confused with specialist vocabulary and key terms because they have not revised them thoroughly enough. Try making your own flashcards with terms and definitions.

Exam practice answers at **www.therevisionbutton.co.uk/myrevisionnotes**

Beliefs about death and beyond

Different beliefs

It is sometimes very difficult to differentiate between a typical 'religious' and 'non-religious view'. This is due to different ideas about the distinction between mind (or soul) and body. Broadly, they fall into two categories: materialist and **dualist**, although there are different interpretations of these terms (see page 69).

There are many different ideas about what death actually is and what, if anything, occurs thereafter. Generally, religions tend to propose some form of afterlife. In contrast, some philosophers and scientists propose that there is nothing beyond death. Religious ideas are often dualist meaning that the body and soul (mind) are in some way separate. Scientists and philosophers who see death as the end of existence, when both the connected mind and body perish, are classified as materialists. Nevertheless, not all religious ideas are dualist in nature, and in the same way, not all scientists and philosophers are materialists – some, such as Alister McGrath and John Polkinghorne, have religious convictions and are persuaded by arguments suggesting the existence of an afterlife. Both categories, however, have followers who *do* believe in an afterlife and so it is not the case that all materialists are atheists. Dualists, nevertheless, believe in an afterlife because the existence of an immortal soul presupposes an afterlife.

> **Dualist** – someone who believes that the mind (soul) and body are separate entities.

Religious and non-religious views

For some, the actual process of death has no significance other than the deterioration and demise of our physical and mental formations. Scientists such as Richard Dawkins and famous atheist philosophers such as Bertrand Russell (1872–1970) take this view. Religions such as Christianity afford death much more significance in terms of it not being intended by God or it not being the end but the mark of a new beginning. According to the New Testament, death is more than just physical. It is about our relationship with God. Death is not some accident of the universe, or something that we will eventually be able to overcome with medical advancement. Death is about a new sphere of life, rather than 'the end'.

Whatever the case may be for the significance of death, funerals – both secular and religious – suggest that it is not without meaning. A religious believer may celebrate life and an exploration of future existence beyond death at a funeral, whereas a secular person may just celebrate life.

Regarding **dualism**, different religions and thinkers have proposed a variety of ways in which the mind or soul survives following the demise of the body. Even as far back as ancient Greece this debate was alive with Plato (c.428–347BCE) and Aristotle taking very different lines of thought. In general, Plato is classed as a dualist whereas Aristotle's understanding of the mind-body relationship is seen to be more materialistic.

> **Dualism** – a fundamental twofold distinction, such as body and soul.

> **Key quote**
>
> 'Aristotle used the one word – psuche – to denote the vital principle that is possessed by every living being.'
>
> (Roger Scruton)

Life after death

There are seemingly many reasons for not believing in life after death.

- Some reasons are similar to those for not believing in God such as a lack of tangible evidence.
- Others reject anything spiritual in nature as no one has ever been able to prove that they have communicated with someone who has died.
- There is also the problem of evil and suffering. Some feel that religious ideas about an afterlife are myths created by human beings to help them feel secure, provide hope and make them less fearful of death.

Even such phenomena as Near Death Experiences (NDEs) have been questioned in terms of verification and meaning. Susan Blackmore (b. 1951) argues that NDEs are not sufficient evidence for the existence of an afterlife because there are alternative explanations, including a biological explanation that cells randomly fire in the visual cortex, giving the illusion of a rapid journey down a tunnel towards a brilliant light.

However, despite this uncertainty, there is still great interest in NDEs as exemplified by Raymond Moody's book *Life After Life* (Rider, 1975), which has been the catalyst for continuing research into the field. Similarly, there has been a growth of interest in the possibility of a 'paranormal' realm, for example, ghosts.

Religious beliefs about the afterlife

Among religions there tend to be two broad categories of ideas: the linear and the cyclic. Linear ideas, such as those within Christianity and Islam, see life as beginning and ending at clear points with a very different afterlife existence. The cyclic, such as Hindu or even Buddhist, suggests a 'recycling' of the soul or energies through reincarnation or **rebirth**.

> **Rebirth** – the Buddhist idea that energies are transferred from one existence to another.

Linear theories

The basic Christian beliefs are as follows:

- There will be a day of judgement, when people will have to account for their past actions.
- There exists a heaven and a hell.
- Jesus will return to Earth and the dead will be resurrected.

In addition, Roman Catholics believe that the souls of those who have not sinned since their last confession will go straight to heaven, while the souls of those who have sinned will go to **purgatory** (a place between heaven and hell) where their souls will be cleansed.

> **Purgatory** – an intermediate place between heaven and hell where the soul goes for purification.

In Christianity, heaven has many interpretations from 'kingdom of God' to 'eternal life'. Paul refers to it as a place (2 Corinthians 5:1) – 'a building from God, an eternal house ... not built by human hands'.

According to the Bible, those who will go to heaven on Judgement Day are the righteous, the persecuted, the sacrificial, Jesus' disciples and those whose names are written in the Lamb's book of life (Revelation 21:27). In general, those who believe in Jesus or those who have been cleansed by the blood of Christ – 'Blessed are those who wash their robes, that they may have the right to the tree of life' (Revelation 22:14) – go to heaven.

In heaven there will be joy, fulfilment and celebration, all in the presence of God. There will also be restoration and the building of a new heaven and Earth.

Hell is described in opposite terms to heaven, for example, it is always 'in depths' rather than 'in heights'. It is dark rather than light. It is a place of silence rather than joy and celebration. Who will go there? According to the Bible, the devil and demons, those whose names were not found written in the book of life, those who do not know God and do not obey the Gospel, and those who do not believe.

The New Testament portrays a Judgement Day 'in the presence of God and of Christ Jesus, who will judge the living and the dead' (2 Timothy 4:1). Both unbelievers and believers will be judged. However, for the believer, 'there is no condemnation for those who are in Christ Jesus' (Romans 8:1). Their judgement is about bestowing various degrees of reward, for example, 'Blessed are you when people insult you ... because great is your reward in heaven' (Matthew 5:11–12).

Cyclic theories

Hinduism is based upon a cyclic view of existence and teaches **reincarnation**, the idea that when you die your soul (atman) still remains and comes back in another body. For Hindus, the soul is an indestructible entity. Reincarnation depends upon a person's **karma**, that is, the actions performed by the individual. If a person has a lot of positive karma, they will have a positive reincarnation of the soul, and vice versa. This cycle of reincarnation has different levels of existence. Hindus believe you can be reincarnated in heavenly and hellish realms. Even the deities are not beyond the reincarnation cycle (samsara) and are ultimately ignorant. All Hindus want to break out of the samsara and believe that it can be escaped (moksha). Hindus reach moksha through various means such as following their religious duty (dharma), being non-violent (ahimsa), building up positive karma and performing worship of the gods (puja). Ultimately, the act of meditation (yoga) is the determining factor for release from samsara to enable a Hindu to become one with Brahman, the ultimate spirit and the only thing beyond the cycle of existence.

> **Reincarnation** – the idea that the eternal essence (soul) discards the body as it survives death but obtains a new body for the next life. It is an idea which is heavily associated with Hinduism and Sikhism.
>
> **Karma** – action that has a moral effect that is either wholesome or not.

Non-religious beliefs about the afterlife

Revised ☐

Non-religious ideas fall exclusively in the category of materialism. The classic statement of materialists can be found in Gilbert Ryle's *The Concept of Mind* (Penguin, 1973). Ryle (1900–1976) argued that the idea of a 'soul' was ill-founded. In creating the idea of a soul we are creating a category that does not exist. He compared it to a search for a 'university' by looking at the individual buildings that compose it, or to a search for team spirit by looking at the members of a team. His famous phrase was that such ideas were 'a ghost in the machine'. In a sense, seeing a soul within a person is like someone who has never seen machinery before believing that there is some 'little person' inside controlling it.

In terms of materialists, there is sometimes a distinction made between 'hard' materialists and 'soft' materialists. For a **hard materialist**, a person's characteristics or personality are no more than physical activities, for example, the idea of consciousness is no more than brain activity. A **soft materialist** accepts that thought processes are more than simple brain activity. Indeed, mind and body are not independent of each other but interact and affect each other. Therefore, physical symptoms can be caused by mental anxieties and processes.

> **Hard materialist** – someone who believes that everything about a human being can be explained by the physical aspect.
>
> **Soft materialist** – someone who believes that the mental processes can interact and affect the physical aspect of a human being.

Areas of uncertainty

Revised

There are some materialistic philosophies that do not draw the conclusion that there is nothing beyond death, despite the strong evidence for a materialistic explanation of death.

The classic example is Buddhism, which is cyclic in nature and therefore similar to Hinduism in terms of human beings having many lives and the idea of escape. However, Buddhists teach rebirth rather than reincarnation, because it is essentially a materialistic philosophy with a key belief that things are 'not-self' and that human beings do not have a soul (anatta).

Like modern psychological materialistic theory, Buddhism proposes that we are just a collection of physical and mental interacting formations (khandhas). At death, there is no single essence or entity that progresses to the next life. Instead, rebirth and reformation (punabhava) of a body in the next life involves a complex transference of karmic energies as outlined famously in the Tibetan Book of The Dead. It describes the six stages of consciousness from life to death and is intended to guide one through the interval between death and the next rebirth (bardo). Rebirth, then, is simply a transferring (or recycling) of the five energies or khandhas. The 'person' reborn is not identical to the one in the previous life, but the same materials have been used!

Another example of a materialist who does not deny an afterlife is John Hick (1922–2012), a famous Christian theologian. His **replica theory**, discussed in his book *Death and Eternal Life* (Westminster/John Knox, 1994), argues that a person can be re-created by God. There is no problem with this logic even if the body and mind (soul) perish at the point of death. God is all-powerful and so can do this. In a sense, this is similar to the Christian teaching of St Paul in 1 Corinthians 15 about the resurrection of a heavenly body.

From the above, it can clearly be seen that not only do ideas about death and beyond vary between religions, science and philosophies, but also that there are clear areas of uncertainty still open to debate.

Replica theory – John Hick's idea that God can instantaneously replicate someone at death into a new existence, despite the old mind and body perishing.

Key quote

'I wish to suggest that we can think of it (the resurrection body) as the divine creation in another space of an exact psycho-physical "replica" of the deceased person.'

(John Hick)

Exam tip

Do not assume that the examiner is familiar with the views of key thinkers; you must explain them thoroughly.

Typical mistake

Some candidates write too much on a topic that is not always relevant to the question.

Now test yourself

Tested

9 What different ideas are there about what happens after death?

10 Why is death significant for Christians?

11 What did Gilbert Ryle argue?

Answers on page 109

Exam practice

(a) Explain religious and secular beliefs about death and beyond.

(45 marks)

(b) 'Life after death is just wishful thinking and has no basis in reality.' Assess this view. (30 marks)

Answers online

Online

Topic III Religious experience

The meaning of the term 'religious experience'

The meaning of the word 'religious' is changing. It is not simply based on theism any more. The growth of interest in '**New Age**' and '**Paganism**' are two diverse elements among the many that now feature in early twenty-first-century ideas.

The meaning of 'experience' is also problematic if it refers to 'directly perceive'. In this case the experience is subjective and private, an inner process that others cannot see. Therefore, there is no way of either verifying or falsifying it. There is also a difficulty in understanding the religious experience since it is private to the person experiencing it and often **ineffable**.

> **New Age** – describes the alternative spiritual subculture interested in such things as meditation, reincarnation, crystals and psychic experience.
>
> **Paganism** – a term covering all the Earth-centred religions; natural religion rather than revealed religion.
>
> **Ineffable** – defies expression; cannot be expressed in words.

Definitions — Revised ☐

There still needs to be a working definition for the term 'religious experience'.

(a) 'An experience that has religious insight.' Usually, the unseen dimensions of existence and God, or Ultimate Reality, is the object of the experience.

(b) A religious experience involves some kind of 'perception' of the invisible world, or involves a perception that some person or thing is a manifestation of the invisible world.

(c) An experience of an event in which one is conscious or aware of some supernatural being/God, or a being related to God, for example, the Virgin Mary, or some indescribable Ultimate Reality.

Hence religious experiences can be theistic (where God is the source and content of the experience) or monistic (where inner being/consciousness is experienced) as monism is the view that all reality is a unity or single substance.

Different types — Revised ☐

General classification

Given the wide variety of experiences, it is not surprising that people have attempted to find some way of grouping them. Caroline Franks Davis has a sixfold listing:

1 Interpretive – for example, answer to prayer.

2 Quasi-sensory – for example, a vision.

3 Revelatory – for example, an 'enlightenment' experience.

4 Regenerative – for example, a conversion.

5 Numinous – for example, experience of God's holiness.

6 Mystical – for example, experience of apprehending Ultimate Reality.

The categories are not mutually exclusive, since an experience may exhibit characteristics of several categories.

There are four main types of religious experiences:

1 Conversion

The word 'conversion' means 'to change direction' or 'to turn around'. It is a broad term and covers a variety of types:

- A unifying of the inner self. This is how the American psychologist and philosopher William James (1842–1910) understood conversion – in psychological terms rather than as a miraculous occurrence. The divided self was an awareness of incompleteness.

- From no religion to a faith. In his book *Confessions*, Augustine (354–430) writes 'it was as though the light of confidence flooded into my heart and all the darkness of doubt was dispelled'.

- From one faith to another. Sundar Singh (1889–1929) was raised as Sikh, then became a Hindu and later became a Christian. He recounts how a light seemed to fill his room and he saw the figure of Jesus saying, 'Why do you persecute me? I died for you.'

- From faith (intellectually believing) to faith (trusting). Martin Luther (1483–1546) is a good example when he realised he was justified by faith (receiving) rather than works (achieving). He discovered that God gave his righteousness as a gift in Christ. Then he was certain of his salvation.

> **Key quote**
>
> 'Conversion is a process of religious change which transforms the way the individual perceives the rest of society and his or her personal place in it, altering one's view of the world.'
>
> (J E McGuire)

Key features

Even though James understood conversion only in psychological terms, he discussed a number of key features of conversion.

- Gradual or sudden – although sudden conversions may have had prior subconscious development.

- Volitional or self-surrendering – giving up personal will, either freely (volitional) or with resistance (self-surrendering).

- Passive or active – either unexpected or someone specifically seeking (for example, through going to an evangelistic meeting).

- Transforming – into a new person; a new creation.

> **Exam tip**
>
> Clearly, not all the features that appear in the various lists occur in every example of a religious experience.

2 Visions

A vision can be defined as something seen other than by ordinary sight – for example, supernatural or prophetic sight experienced in sleep or ecstasy – especially when it conveys a revelation.

The different types of vision include:

- Group – for example, Angels of Mons. During the First World War a vision of St George and a phantom bowman halted the Kaiser's troops. Others claimed angels had thrown a protective curtain around the British troops saving them from disaster.

- Individual – for example, Bernadette of Lourdes claimed to have been instructed by an apparition of the Virgin Mary to dig a hole for a healing spring to appear.

- **Corporeal** – external but only visible to certain people, for example, appearances of angels.

- Imaginative – for example, John's visions of strange creatures in the book of Revelation. Dreams are also sometimes considered to be visions and can be categorised under this type.

> **Corporeal** – of a material nature, physical.

Exam practice answers at **www.therevisionbutton.co.uk/myrevisionnotes**

Form

The form and content of visions may include:

- an image or event in which there is a message, for example, Peter's vision of the large sheet descending (Acts 10:9–16)
- religious figures, for example, St Teresa of Avila's most famous vision was of an angel holding a long spear with something like fire on the end. This seemed to pierce her heart several times and when it was withdrawn it left her 'completely afire with a great love for God'
- places, for example, Guru Nanak's vision of God's court in which he was escorted into God's presence and commanded to drink a cup of nectar
- fantastic creatures/figures, for example, Ezekiel's vision of four living creatures (Ezekiel 1:5–14) – each had a face of a man, and on the right side had the face of a lion, and on the left the face of an ox; each also had the face of an eagle
- final judgement/end of world, for example, John's visions of final judgement in the book of Revelation (Revelation 20:12–15) – anyone's name that was not found in the book of life was thrown into the lake of fire.

Now test yourself

Tested ☐

1   List four types of conversion experience.
2   List four key features of conversion experiences.
3   List four types of vision.

Answers on page 109

> **Key quote**
>
> '… he appeared to be one of the highest types of angels who seem to be all afire … in his hands I saw a long golden spear and at the end of the iron tip I seemed to see a point of fire. With this he seemed to pierce my heart several times so that it penetrated to my entrails. When he drew it out … he left me completely afire with a great love for God.'
>
> (Teresa of Avila)

3 Revelation   Revised ☐

Revelation is divine self-disclosure. Through revelation, the divine becomes known to humanity. Like visions, revelation can be an aspect of any of the types of religious experience.

Main features

- Sudden and of short duration.
- Alleged new knowledge acquired immediately.
- Alleged new knowledge comes from external agent.
- The alleged new knowledge is received with utter conviction.
- The insights are often impossible to put into words (ineffability).

Content

- Universal truths – for example, Guru Nanak received a universal truth revelation about the name of God.
- The future – for example, Hildegard of Bingen (1098–1179) claimed to have received insight from God about the sixteenth-century Protestant Reformation.
- The present – for example, Benny Hinn, a well-known leader in the charismatic movement, claims he has words of knowledge from God.
- Spiritual help – for example, when reading Scripture receiving a deeper understanding of God.

Propositional or non-propositional

- Propositional refers to the communication of some truth by God through supernatural means. The content of this revelation is a body of truths expressed in statements or propositions – for example, in Islam the Prophet Muhammad received the Qur'an.

- Non-propositional refers to the moment of 'realisation' coming at the end of a period of reflection, for example, Buddhist Scriptures emerged from the Buddha himself rather than from some transcendent source.

4 Mystical Revised ☐

Mysticism can be defined as an experience that alters the state of consciousness and brings people to claim a new awareness of ultimate reality. For theists, it is usually union and communion with God. For followers of Eastern religions, it is usually a realisation of enlightenment.

Type

The academic Robert Zaehner (1913–1974) distinguishes three types:

- Nature – God can be experienced through the natural world as He is everywhere. For example, Alfred Lord Tennyson described his mystic experiences – 'individuality itself seemed to dissolve and fade away into boundless being'.

- Monistic – the experience of one's own spirit as the Absolute, the identity of Atman and Brahman. Found more in Eastern traditions and particularly taught by eighth-century Indian sage Shankara. The goal is the realisation of one's own identity with the Absolute Reality, so that you become that Absolute.

- Theistic – union or communion with a personal Lord. Theistic mystics speak about having a consciousness of being fully absorbed into or even identical with God. The French abbott, Bernard of Clairvaux (1090–1153) described this unification as a 'mutuality of love'.

> **Exam tip**
> It is important to show that there is diversity within mysticism, for example, nature, monistic, theistic.

Walter Stace (1886–1967), a British philosopher, distinguishes two types:

- Extrovertive (outward looking) – where the plurality of objects in the world are transfigured into a single living entity. 'I saw that the universe is not composed of dead matter, but is, on the contrary, a living Presence.' (Richard Bucke, psychologist)

- Introvertive (inward looking) – where a person loses their identity as a separate individual and merges slowly into the divine unity. 'It is pure unitary consciousness wherein awareness of the world and of multiplicity is completely obliterated. It is ineffable peace. It is the Supreme Good. It is One without a second. It is the Self.' (The Upanishads)

Key features

William James identified four features of mysticism:

1 Ineffability – the experience defies expression. Phrases such as 'the dissolution of the personal ego' are empty to those who have not experienced such things.

2 Noetic quality – states that allow apparent insight into the depths of truths unobtainable by the intellect alone. They have a force of certainty and reality.

3 Transiency – states that cannot be maintained for long periods of time. Though the states are remembered, they are imperfectly recalled. Usually they leave the recipient with a profound sense of the importance of the experience.

4 Passivity – the recipient feels they are being taken over by a superior power.

The philosopher F C Happold identified another three characteristics.

1 Consciousness of the oneness of everything. The usual awareness of identity, or ego, fades away and the person becomes aware of being part of a dimension much greater than themselves. This unity can be introvertive, where external sense impressions are left behind, or extrovertive, where the person reports that they feel a part of everything that is (that is, all is one).

2 Sense of timelessness. The subject feels in a realm of eternity or infinity – beyond past, present and future, and beyond ordinary three-dimensional space.

3 The idea that the ego is not the real 'I'. There is an unchanging self that is immortal and that lies behind the usual experience of self.

The Italian medieval theologian and philosopher St Bonaventure identified three stages of a mystic experience:

1 Purgative stage – the mystic is purified and prepared for the experience through meditation.

2 Illuminative stage – the mystic is affected both in their intellect and feelings.

3 Unitive stage – the mystic gains a continuing union with the Divine.

The numinous
Revised

The German theologian Rudolf Otto (*The Idea of the Holy*, Oxford University Press, 1958 (first published 1917)) argued there was one common factor to all religious experience – the numinous. Religious experience is about a feeling – an experience of the holy. It is something 'wholly other' than the natural world and beyond apprehension and comprehension, and includes:

- awefulness – inspiring awe, a sort of profound unease
- overpoweringness – inspires a feeling of humility
- energy/urgency – creating an impression of immense vigour, compelling
- wholly other – totally outside normal experience
- fascination – causes the subject of the experience to be caught up in it.

A good example of the numinous is the experience of Moses at the Burning Bush (Exodus 3:6).

Now test yourself

4 List five main features of revelatory experiences.

5 Explain the difference between propositional and non-propositional.

6 List the three types of mystical experiences that Robert Zaehner identified.

7 List the three characteristics of mystical experiences that Happold identified.

Answers on page 109

Tested

The influence of religious experience

Source of religious practice
Revised

Religious practice includes ritual, ceremonies, festivals and way of life. The correct performance of the ritual is vital, as is the need for purity in order to participate. Rites of passage are the means by which many people encounter religion directly. The main religious rites of passage correspond to the stages of life: birth/naming, becoming an adult/initiation, marriage and burial.

Religious practices can also be based around a religious experience. Often, these have been further developed well beyond the original. Many festivals are celebrations of a past event that involved a religious experience. For example, during Ramadan, Muslims celebrate the time when the verses of the Qur'an were revealed to the Prophet Muhammad.

Sources of good religious behaviour

Revised

One of the common themes in a conversion experience is the sense of a new being, a transforming process, a rejection of the old life and a desire for a new purer life. As a result of this change, a new lifestyle is required. The new standards of behaviour (usually contained in the Scriptures) will reflect the teaching of the faith into which the person has converted.

A religious experience can bring a person into a faith so that the person feels the ethical standards of the religion have new authority and are to be followed. A religious experience can also empower the believer to live this new ethical life.

Key quotes

'Therefore, if anyone is in Christ, he is a new creation; the old has gone, the new has come.'

(2 Corinthians 5:17)

'Be imitators of God, therefore … and live a life of love … But among you there must not be even a hint of sexual immorality, or of any kind of impurity, or of greed, because these are improper for God's holy people.'

(Ephesians 5:1–3)

Value of religious experience

Revised

As historical events

The world's major religions each record their founder having some sort of religious experience – for example, the Buddha as he sat under the Bodhi tree, or Guru Nanak's (Sikhism) revelation about the name of God (the Mool Mantra). These religious experiences, as historical events, are often seen as validations as to the truth of a particular religion.

As ongoing present-day experiences

It seems that religious experience can lead people into faith – for example, they may have a sudden feeling that God is there with them, and they believe. Equally, faith can lead people into a religious experience – for example, a convert may have some sort of religious experience as they worship and pray.

Believers also maintain that God is at work in the world and thus have ongoing experiences of God. Shared worship can lead to a special kind of communal experience. The reading and preaching of the sacred text can be the trigger for religious experience – for example, Muslims, Hindus and Christians all consider their Scriptures to be the revealed word of God. Through these texts and others, it is believed that God speaks to the individual.

Typical mistake

A common mistake is to list examples of good religious behaviour but then fail to explain how these examples are derived from a particular or distinct religious experience.

Contribution of religious experience

Foundation for particular religions

In most religions there is often a central pivotal figure linked to the founding of that religion. Usually these figures experience a particularly significant event that marks the start of their ministry. It is a turning point often followed by a period of doubt and reflection in which they prepare themselves for their mission. For example, Abraham is a foundation figure in Judaism. His call from God to leave Ur and the establishing of the **covenant** is recorded in Genesis 12.

Covenant – an agreement between God and human beings.

Other figures who have had a religious experience and so have been instrumental in starting religious movements include Martin Luther (Protestants/Lutherans) and John Wesley (Methodists).

Source of faith for individual religious people

When a believer states they believe in Jesus, they usually mean more than just belief that Jesus was an historical figure. It also implies trust in Jesus. This 'belief in' conveys an attitude of commitment, trust or loyalty on the part of the believer. For many people this move from belief in an objective fact to an attitude of trust is often brought about by a personal religious experience. Clearly, the religious experience of conversion is central.

Contribution to religious faith as a whole

Other people's religious experience can act as an encouragement or strengthening of faith. Paul referred to his religious conversion on the road to Damascus to encourage others to believe. In evangelistic meetings, believers often give an account ('testimony') of their own conversion and experiences of God to encourage others.

Exam tip

Try to obtain a copy of the assessment objectives and the levels of response to refer to, so that you know what is expected in order to gain a level 5 or beyond.

Now test yourself

8 Give one way in which religious experience can be a source of good religious behaviour.
9 Explain the difference between 'belief that' and 'belief in'.
10 Explain how people's religious experience can be of value to others.

Answers on page 109

Validity of religious experience

Verification

This is problematic as religious experiences are usually private, rather than public, and it is not possible therefore to 'check' someone's religious experience.

Subjective – having its source within the mind.

The problem	Why it is a problem	Possible responses
Religious experiences are not the same as sense experiences.	God is not material. God does not have a definite location. How would you recognise it was God you were experiencing?	Just as we are known to each other by a kind of awareness of the mind rather than through the physical body, so in the same way we may be able to experience a non-physical God.
A direct experience of God is impossible.	The finite cannot experience the infinite. Our senses detect objects in time and space. God is not such an object.	How do we know God cannot enter into time and space? It is reasonable to believe God would seek interaction.
A religious experience cannot be verified.	Because religious experience is **subjective**, it is impossible for someone else to verify that event since they have no access to it.	What about shared religious experiences? There may be criteria that would add weight to validity (for example, the experience makes a noticeable difference to the religious life of the person). Swinburne (b. 1934) argues the onus is on the sceptic to show the experience is delusive.
There is a lack of uniformity in religious experiences.	The messages, visions, information and beliefs apparently transmitted are so diverse and contradictory that it is impossible for the majority of religious experiences to be real and accurate.	God may reveal himself in terms of cultural beliefs that we will understand and interpret. Different experiences recounted do not mean they are all in error. Maybe only one religion is correct so other religious experiences are false, but those of that one religion are true.
There are various natural explanations for religious experiences.	(a) Drugs such as hallucinogens have been linked to religious experiences.	The neurological changes associated with religious experiences may mean the brain perceives a spiritual reality rather than causes those experiences.
	(b) Stimulation of the temporal lobes produces altered perception akin to religious experiences.	This may not induce the experience but facilitate it. It is difficult to isolate the cause from the effect.
	(c) Brain imaging shows certain regions of the brain are active during religious experiences (for example, Andrew Newberg studied the brains of Franciscan nuns during prayer, Tibetan monks during meditation and Pentecostals speaking in tongues, and found that the brain activity was similar in each case).	Just because we can explain religious experiences through science it does not necessarily rule out divine activity.
	(d) Isolation and sensory deprivation may explain religious experiences of holy people living in some sort of wilderness.	Deprivation may help to 'fine-tune' our spiritual awareness.
	(e) Personality traits – people with a particular personality trait (a 'feeling' person rather than a 'thinking' person) will be likely to be drawn to religious belief.	Religious believers include all types of personality traits.
	(f) Carl Jung – the source of religious experience is the psyche. Part of our psyche contains structures that are image-creating. These are called archetypes. The God archetype generates religious images. A religious experience is an indirect encounter with the God archetype.	Jung's theory of archetypes can be more simply explained by how all human beings share similar experiences.

Value for religious community

Revised

Accounts of religious experiences can be of value to the religious community. For example, religious experiences can:

- affirm people's faith as the religious community hear of God present and active in other people's lives
- provide a focus for the religious community, such as the visions at Lourdes making it a centre for Roman Catholic pilgrimage
- inspire members of the religious community to develop their own spiritual life, as they seek to have similar experiences
- reveal messages from God that can be shared with the religious community, such as words of knowledge claimed by some charismatics or even predictions of the end of the world.

Value for an individual

Revised

If an individual has a religious experience, then the value of that religious experience to that individual may include:

- inspiring compassionate and/or new standards of behaviour (indeed, one of Theresa of Avila's tests for an authentic religious experience was a positive change in behaviour in the person)
- revealing or confirming a sense of what life means, particularly one's own life
- bringing to faith or confirming and strengthening one's existing faith.

Clearly, religious experiences can also cause doubts and concerns. For example, what does an adherent of one faith think about religious experiences claimed by a member of a different faith? What if the religious experience is seen as a sign of a spiritual life, but not everyone has the religious experience – are they truly spiritual? For example, some charismatics claim speaking in tongues is a sign of baptism in the Holy Spirit.

> **Typical mistake**
>
> A common mistake is to only give examples from one religion. It is expected that candidates will know something of both Eastern and Western traditions.

> **Now test yourself**
>
> Tested
>
> 11 If religious experiences are authentic, how can one account for the lack of uniformity of religious experiences?
> 12 Why might some religious experiences cause doubts and concerns to a religious believer?
>
> Answers on page 109

> **Exam practice**
>
> **(a)** Explain what is meant by the term 'a religious experience'. (45 marks)
> **(b)** 'Religious experiences are of little value since they cannot be verified.' To what extent do you agree with this claim? (30 marks)
>
> **Answers online**
>
> Online

Now test yourself: answers

Unit 3A: 1 Libertarianism, free will and determinism

1   Free will enables moral responsibility.

2   Genetics may influence our actions (internal causation) or alternatively it could be our environment (external causation), for example, our upbringing.

3   Willpower enables a person to act appropriately by restraining immoral urges.

4   Our experiences tell us that we do make choices in life.

5   Total freedom and absolutely no determinism.

6   Personality explains the mental and physical processes of a human being, but the moral self illustrates how there is another aspect of autonomy for the will of an individual to allow freedom of choice.

7   As an illusion – just like the person who awakes in a locked room and 'decides' to stay.

8   Causality: the idea that any action is linked and determined or influenced by some cause directly and completely.

9   There must be some autonomy of the will otherwise reward and punishment would be unjust and this would contradict God's attributes.

10 The absolute rule of God over human will, because God has already established what will happen.

11 Any two points from the following list:
    ● Libertarianism recognises moral responsibility and this also encourages people to seek behaviour that is constructive and meaningful to society.
    ● It explains the moral diversity of our world given the fact that different people will make different decisions.
    ● The belief in free will justifies reward and punishment sanctions and 'makes sense' of things, justifying the parameters of our societies and legal systems.

12 Any two points from the following list:
    ● Libertarianism does not recognise the finding of science that everything is determined and interconnected.
    ● Libertarianism does not allow for conditioning of behaviour when scientific experiments demonstrate that this occurs.
    ● Libertarianism cannot explain why actions and behaviour are chaotic if uncaused.
    ● Libertarianism has the problem that there is conflict when one person's liberty opposes the freedom of another person, meaning that no one can be said to have true liberty.

2 Virtue ethics

1   It concerns itself with the person, not a rule or a consequence of an action.

2   In his *Nichomachean Ethics*.

3   A moral virtue is developed by practice whereas an intellectual virtue is taught.

4   Wisdom and justice.

5   The vices of excess and deficiency.

6   Because it studied ethics in abstract, out of its social and historical context.

7   The bureaucratic manager, rich aesthete and therapist.

8   Foot sees pride as a vice like Aquinas, and she sees wisdom as both intellectual and moral.

9   Because Aristotle himself uses it as an example in his book.

10 Liberality and magnificence.

11 Any two from the table on page 26.

12 Any two from the table on page 26.

3 Religious views on sexual behaviour and human relationships

1   As Genesis 2:24 confirms, heterosexual relationships and heterosexual marriages are the norm according to Scripture.

2   The Roman Catholic Church sees marriage as being for procreation; the Anglican view is that it is a mystical union.

3   'Avoid sexual immorality' (1 Thessalonians 4:3); 'You shall not commit adultery' (Exodus 20:14) or other suitable quotes can be used to support the scripture-based teaching that promiscuity, adultery and sex outside marriage are disapproved of.

4   Monks abstain from sex; some Christians may see a couple living together as upholding Christian teachings.

5   Galatians 3:28 and the examples of the stories of Ruth or Esther. Galatians teaches all are equal. The examples of Ruth and Esther demonstrate that it can be argued that women have a significant impact upon religion.

6   The Roman Catholic Church does not allow female priests; the Anglican Church does not allow female bishops despite a recent vote by the Synod (although the view is that it is to be discussed again at a later stage). Traditional views regarding family ('breadwinning' for men and raising children for women) but depends upon tradition followed.

7   Leviticus 20:13, Genesis 2:24 or Romans 1:27 can be used as examples which show disapproval of homosexuality. Some may point to the relationship between David and Jonathan which is very close and then use this to support homosexual relationships because the Bible states that David loved Jonathan more than he loved women (2 Samuel 1:26).

8   The Roman Catholic tradition rejects the act; the Anglican Church allows non-practising homosexuals to enter civil partnerships.

9 Love – St Paul and agape or Old Testament and hesed. Family – Exodus 20:12 and extended families of the Old Testament.

10 The ideal of the traditional nuclear family and the recognition of alternative families, e.g. reconstituted.

11 Any two from table on page 39.

12 Any two from table on page 39.

13 Any two from the table on page 39.

4 Science and technology

1 Much research is repetitive and pointless.

2 Any from the table on page 42.

3 Singer argues that animals should have the same rights as human beings and that to experiment on them is speciesism.

4 Animals do not have souls.

5 That human beings either rule over them or have responsibility for looking after them.

6 It is the lesser of two evils because the benefits for human beings outweigh the cost for animals.

7 Drug trials, behaviour studies and medical treatments (observation of).

8 He discovered penicillin.

9 By ensuring that there is no psychological damage and assessing the ethical nature of the activity.

10 *Jus ad bellum* concerns conduct before war while *jus in bello* concerns conduct during war.

11 'You shall not kill' (Ten Commandments) and Jesus saying 'he who lives by the sword will die by the sword'.

12 The Human Fertilisation and Embryology Authority (HFEA) strictly regulates the work into embryo research.

13 AID is insemination by donor and this would mean adultery.

14 The Universal Declaration of Human Rights.

15 Liberty (founded 1934) is a movement that aims to protect an individual's freedoms and rights in line with the UDHR.

16 Any points from the list below:
- History teaches us that science and technology do need controlling, for example, the terrible experimentation by the Nazis.
- We need to protect society from any further abuse.
- No control would mean 'anything goes' and create chaos, immoral activity and the use of science and technology could get out of control.
- We must think about the future of our planet.
- Ethical theories provide clear guidance and most agree on technology issues so it would be an effective way of avoiding all the potential problems.

17 Any point from the list below:
- Can the potential use and development of nuclear power be taken away now that it has been discovered?
- Can we eradicate knowledge and move backwards? It is highly unlikely because somebody, somewhere will use it.
- To try to 'undiscover' things is dangerous because it leaves the possibility that someone will abuse it and so it is best to embrace new knowledge and control it ethically.

18 Any point from the list below:
- There has been a great history of religious involvement in ethical issues.
- It is vital because ethical issues are fundamental to religion.
- God directs religious views and so it has to be right for religion to be involved.
- Much religious involvement is from an ethical perspective.
- Secular control can be driven by materialism.

Unit 3B: 1 The ontological argument: faith and reason

1 A being than which nothing greater can be conceived.

2 The conclusion is shown to follow from the premises.

3 A contingent being need not be or could be different. A necessary being could not not be, that is, it has to be.

4 God is a different order of being. The ontological argument is only applicable to the existence of God.

5 (i) Anselm does not have a theory of absolute objective greatness, whereas Descartes does have a theory of absolute objective perfection.
(ii) For Anselm, existence does not add to the concept of God. Rather the focus is on existing in reality as opposed to existing as an idea. However, for Descartes, existence does add to the concept of God. Existence is a necessary addition to the concept of something that is perfect, since part of perfection is existence.

6 (a) This is logically inconsistent and is therefore not a possible world.
(b) There is no logical inconsistency. It is a possible world though many may regard it as unlikely!
(c) This is our present world so it must therefore be possible.

7 God is beyond human understanding. Therefore we have no way of knowing if our definition of God is correct.

8 Existence does add greatness – real money permits the purchase of real items in the real world.

9 (i) God is unique since he has necessary existence. Therefore, deriving an existential claim from a definition only works for the definition of God.
(ii) Concept and actuality are related – for example, round squares cannot exist. Therefore, you can move to actuality from a concept.

10 In the first statement, the understanding will lead to belief. In the second statement the person already believes and their belief will lead them to understanding.

11 The ontological argument is a deductive argument and therefore appeals to logic and reason. Therefore, if the premises are true the conclusion follows and would lead to a universal proof.

12 Stephen Davis suggests that concept and actuality are related (see page 55). This implies Gaunilo's criticism is flawed.

2 Religious language

1 It is used to describe things that are over and beyond our world, so that people are no longer sure what is being communicated.

2 Empiricism, science and Wittgenstein's picture theory.

3 Meaningful – the statement has meaning. Meaning – what the statement is conveying or signifying.

4 The strong form demands verification in practice and conclusively. The weak form demands only that the verification is in principle and probable.

5 If a statement could be shown to be false, then the statement is meaningful.

6 Statements such as 'God is good' or 'God does miracles' cannot be falsified.

7 Hare wanted to show that although religious language statements could not be shown to be true or false since they were not literal, they were still important because of the result they had on our conduct.

8 Eschatological verification claims that life after death is open to weak verification, since if it is true you could experience it.

9 The analogy of proportion and the analogy of attribution.

10 In Wittgenstein's picture theory he argued that words stemmed from objects. In his idea of language games, he saw language as functional. It is not so much about meaning but about context.

11 (i) It does not show that religious language is meaningless since verification is possible (for example, eschatological verification).

(ii) The VP cannot itself be verified. It fails its own test.

12 Two from the following:

(i) Some non-falsifiable statements are still regarded as meaningful (for example, toys in cupboard that only come out at night when no one can see them).

(ii) The FP cannot itself be falsified. It fails its own test.

(iii) The science paradigm is inappropriate for religious language.

13 There is no way to judge whether a symbol gives the correct insights about the ultimate.

3 Body, soul and personal identity

1 Incorporeal, immortal essence of a person, capable of union with the divine, that which animates the body and gives it life.

2 The 'use' argument, the 'recollection' argument and the 'opposites' argument.

3 Dualism suggests that the body and soul are two distinct and separate substances while materialism suggests that the body and soul are the same substance.

4 (a) Resurrection (usually bodily) is about being raised from the dead, brought back to life (in Christian teaching – resurrected with a new body in a new spiritual realm). Reincarnation is about the transmigration of the soul into a new body in this world.

(b) The difference concerns that element that is reborn. In reincarnation it is a fixed entity (like a soul) but in rebirth the identification is more akin to a stream of consciousness.

5 It seeks to resolve the problem of reconciling the ideas of life after death and personal identity with a materialist view of the universe.

6 (a) Evidence for Jesus' resurrection.

(b) Remembered lives, often by means of hypnosis.

7 (a) Moody wrote *Life After Life*, which popularised the idea of NDEs. He also coined the phrase NDE.

(b) Fenwick is a British psychiatrist who identified the key features of NDEs and researched evidence to support the occurrence of NDEs.

8 The soul–body dualism (something can survive that is not physical); the existence of a spiritual realm (a realm after death where life is lived); the experience of judgement (suggests a continuity between this life and life after death).

9 Cultural differences help a person understand what is happening, rather than imagination, for example, medieval accounts refer to crossing a test bridge over a fiery river, while modern accounts refer to crossing a border. The idea of a test bridge would have been understood in medieval times. However, it does raise doubts about NDEs since one would have thought that the experience of the afterlife would be the same in any culture or generation.

10 Children would be unaware of the classic reported features of NDEs and of relatives who had died. Therefore, their citing of such details suggest that their experiences were authentic.

4 The problem of evil

1 The logical problem involves highlighting the apparent logical contradiction between the existence of God and the existence of evil. The evidential problem of evil is about weighing up probabilities based on the evidence. What is more likely given the existence of evil – God or no God?

2 Free beings have the possibility to act in an evil way. Because they are free, there is no guarantee they will not, at some point, act in an evil way.

3 It is called soul-deciding because a person's response to evil decides the ultimate destination of their soul after death.

4 To make truly moral decisions there must be consequences to our actions. The larger the consequences the more we can make significant moral choices.

5 Epistemic distance gives ambiguity to the world so we can choose freely and develop.

6 It is called the 'vale of soul-making' because the theodicy argues that the environment of our world is ideal for the development of our soul.

7 The Augustinian-type theodicies seem to focus on the afterlife. They imply that God is unaffected by our suffering and the world and that our experiences are unimportant. All that matters is salvation and escaping from this world. In

contrast, process theodicy puts the focus back onto this life and our experiences in the here and now.

8 People must be free to choose. Also some argue for annihilation rather than hell.

9 Jesus and his death are seen as an inspiring example. The death of Jesus plays no part in the theodicy other than Jesus being an example. The theodicy would be unaffected if Jesus never existed. This is very different from the Augustinian theodicy, which centres on the death of Jesus as a necessity for salvation.

10 (a) In process theodicy, God is not omnipotent.

    (b) Because process theodicy fits in with modern evolutionary theories. God is also seen as a co-sufferer and intimately involved in this universe.

11 Two from the following:

    (i) Why didn't God create beings that always freely choose to do right?

    (ii) Where did the temptation to do evil come from?

    (iii) How loving is God if he created human beings knowing the pain and suffering they would experience?

    (iv) Is free will a coherent concept?

    (v) Surely God could reduce the amount of suffering by intervening on occasions?

12 Two from the following:

    (i) Human beings are part of the created world. Therefore natural evil could be related to human action.

    (ii) Natural evil is necessary to produce second-order goods.

    (iii) Natural evil is only evil when it causes suffering.

13 Augustinian theodicy: accepts authority of Scripture; evil not created by God; explains natural evil.

    Free-will defence: God is not responsible for evil.

    Hick's 'vale of soul-making': consistent with evolutionary theories; evil is justified as all achieve the goal of heaven.

    Process theodicy: consistent with evolutionary theories; God is co-sufferer; removes logical problem of evil by rejecting God as omnipotent.

Unit 4A: Topic I Life, death and beyond

1 Human beings have souls.

2 Research to find how our mind is determined by the physical coding of our bodies, that is, the physical origins of all mental activity.

3 They say it is an illusion, Ryle called it a 'ghost in the machine'.

4 Eschatology is general religious teaching about the end days, but apocalyptic material is that which is specifically 'revealed' to an individual, usually through a vision.

5 They are dramatic, full of conflict, include hardships, evil and despair with an ultimate battle between good and evil.

6 It is the whole purpose of human life.

7 Preparation, reward and punishment.

8 NDE, ghosts and the paranormal, the idea of the mind (or soul) being separate from the body.

9 Resurrection, different existences, spiritual existence, rebirth, reincarnation, replica.

10 It makes the statement that the relationship between God and humanity has broken down.

11 He argued that the soul is a mere illusion like a 'ghost in the machine'.

Unit 4A: Topic III Religious experience

1 Unifying of inner self; no religion to a faith; one faith to another faith; from intellectual faith to a trusting faith.

2 Gradual/sudden; volitional/self-surrendering; passive/active; transforming.

3 Group; individual; corporeal; imaginative.

4 Sudden; new knowledge acquired; new knowledge from external agent; utterly convinced; ineffability.

5 Propositional is to do with a body of truths expressed in statements whereas non-propositional includes attitudes and opinions and is a moment of realisation. Non-propositional is not communication through supernatural means, whereas propositional is.

6 Nature; monistic; theistic.

7 Consciousness of the oneness of everything; sense of timelessness; idea that the ego is not the real 'I'.

8 Conversion experiences bring a sense of a new life.

9 'Belief that' expresses belief in some fact; 'belief in' expresses an attitude of trust, commitment or loyalty.

10 It can act as an encouragement or strengthening of faith.

11 Differences enable the person to understand and interpret the different ways God makes himself known to different people in different cultures. Maybe only one religion is correct so the other religious experiences are false, but those of that one religion are true.

12 They may lead a believer to be concerned that members of other faiths claim religious experiences, and to ask which is correct. Also, not having the religious experience that one should expect to have as the sign of a spiritual state (for example, speaking in tongues is thought by some to be the sign of the baptism in the Holy Spirit).

Notes

Exam practice answers at **www.therevisionbutton.co.uk/myrevisionnotes**